MACMILLAN MASTER GUIDES

GENERAL EDITOR: JAMES GIBSON

Published

JANE AUSTEN	*Emma* ... *Sense and ...* *Pride and Prejudice* Raymond Wilson *Mansfield Park* Richard Wirdnam
SAMUEL BECKETT	*Waiting for Godot* Jennifer Birkett
WILLIAM BLAKE	*Songs of Innocence* and *Songs of Experience* Alan Tomlinson
ROBERT BOLT	*A Man for all Seasons* Leonard Smith
EMILY BRONTË	*Wuthering Heights* Hilda D. Spear
GEOFFREY CHAUCER	*The Miller's Tale* Michael Alexander *The Pardoner's Tale* Geoffrey Lester *The Prologue to the Canterbury Tales* Nigel Thomas and Richard Swan
CHARLES DICKENS	*Bleak House* Dennis Butts *Great Expectations* Dennis Butts *Hard Times* Norman Page
GEORGE ELIOT	*Middlemarch* Graham Handley *Silas Marner* Graham Handley *The Mill on the Floss* Helen Wheeler
HENRY FIELDING	*Joseph Andrews* Trevor Johnson
E. M. FORSTER	*Howards End* Ian Milligan *A Passage to India* Hilda D. Spear
WILLIAM GOLDING	*The Spire* Rosemary Sumner *Lord of the Flies* Raymond Wilson
OLIVER GOLDSMITH	*She Stoops to Conquer* Paul Ranger
THOMAS HARDY	*The Mayor of Casterbridge* Ray Evans *Tess of the d'Urbervilles* James Gibson *Far from the Madding Crowd* Colin Temblett-Wood
JOHN KEATS	*Selected Poems* John Garrett
PHILIP LARKIN	*The Whitsun Weddings* and *The Less Deceived* Andrew Swarbrick
D. H. LAWRENCE	*Sons and Lovers* R. P. Draper
HARPER LEE	*To Kill a Mockingbird* Jean Armstrong
CHRISTOPHER MARLOWE	*Doctor Faustus* David A. Male
THE METAPHYSICAL POETS	Joan van Emden

MACMILLAN MASTER GUIDES

THOMAS MIDDLETON and WILLIAM ROWLEY	*The Changeling* Tony Bromham
ARTHUR MILLER	*The Crucible* Leonard Smith
GEORGE ORWELL	*Animal Farm* Jean Armstrong
WILLIAM SHAKESPEARE	*Richard II* Charles Barber *Hamlet* Jean Brooks *King Lear* Francis Casey *Henry V* Peter Davison *The Winter's Tale* Diana Devlin *Julius Caesar* David Elloway *Macbeth* David Elloway *Measure for Measure* Mark Lilly *Henry IV Part I* Helen Morris *Romeo and Juliet* Helen Morris *The Tempest* Kenneth Pickering *A Midsummer Night's Dream* Kenneth Pickering
GEORGE BERNARD SHAW	*St Joan* Leonée Ormond
RICHARD SHERIDAN	*The School for Scandal* Paul Ranger *The Rivals* Jeremy Rowe
ALFRED TENNYSON	*In Memoriam* Richard Gill
JOHN WEBSTER	*The White Devil* and *The Duchess of Malfi* David A. Male

Forthcoming

CHARLOTTE BRONTË	*Jane Eyre* Robert Miles
JOHN BUNYAN	*The Pilgrim's Progress* Beatrice Batson
JOSEPH CONRAD	*The Secret Agent* Andrew Mayne
T. S. ELIOT	*Murder in the Cathedral* Paul Lapworth *Selected Poems* Andrew Swarbrick
GERARD MANLEY HOPKINS	*Selected Poems* R. Watt
BEN JONSON	*Volpone* Michael Stout
RUDYARD KIPLING	*Kim* Leonée Ormond
ARTHUR MILLER	*Death of a Salesman* Peter Spalding
JOHN MILTON	*Comus* Tom Healy
WILLIAM SHAKESPEARE	*Othello* Tony Bromham *As You Like It* Kiernan Ryan *Coriolanus* Gordon Williams *Antony and Cleopatra* Martin Wine
ANTHONY TROLLOPE	*Barchester Towers* Ken Newton
VIRGINIA WOOLF	*To the Lighthouse* John Mepham *Mrs Dalloway* Julian Pattison
W. B. YEATS	*Selected Poems* Stan Smith

MACMILLAN MASTER GUIDES
THE PARDONER'S TALE
BY GEOFFREY CHAUCER

GEOFFREY LESTER

MACMILLAN
EDUCATION

First edition 1987

Published by
MACMILLAN EDUCATION LTD
Houndmills, Basingstoke, Hampshire RG21 2XS
and London
Companies and representatives
throughout the world

Printed in Hong Kong

British Library Cataloguing in Publication Data
Lester, Geoff
The pardoner's tale by Geoffrey Chaucer.
—(Macmillan master guides)
1. Chaucer, Geoffrey. Pardoner's tale
I. Title   II. Chaucer, Geoffrey
821'.1   PR1868.P3
ISBN 0–333–42227–9 Pbk
ISBN 0–333–42228–7 Pbk export

CONTENTS

GENERAL EDITOR'S PREFACE

The aim of the Macmillan Master Guides is to help you to appreciate the book you are studying by providing information about it and by suggesting ways of reading and thinking about it which will lead to a fuller understanding. The section on the writer's life and background has been designed to illustrate those aspects of the writer's life which have influenced the work, and to place it in its personal and literary context. The summaries and critical commentary are of special importance in that each brief summary of the action is followed by an examination of the significant critical points. The space which might have been given to repetitive explanatory notes has been devoted to a detailed analysis of the kind of passage which might confront you in an examination. Literary criticism is concerned with both the broader aspects of the work being studied and with its detail. The ideas which meet us in reading a great work of literature, and their relevance to us today, are an essential part of our study, and our Guides look at the thought of their subject in some detail. But just as essential is the craft with which the writer has constructed his work of art, and this may be considered under several technical headings − characteris-ation, language, style and stagecraft, for example.

The authors of these Guides are all teachers and writers of wide experience, and they have chosen to write about books they admire and know well in the belief that they can communicate their admiration to you. But you yourself must read and know intimately the book you are studying. No one can do that for you. You should see this book as a lamp-post. Use it to shed light, not to lean against. If you know your text and know what it is saying about life, and how it says it, then you will enjoy it, and there is no better way of passing an examination in literature.

JAMES GIBSON

Acknowledgement

Cover illustration: *Royal Manuscript*, a miniature taken from a volume of John Lydgate's poems, depicting Lydgate and the Canterbury pilgrims leaving Canterbury, flemish style.

Photograph © The British Library London and reproduced by courtesy of the Bridgeman Art Library.

NOTE ON THE LINE

NUMBERING

The line numberings used in this book are from the standard edition
of Chaucer's complete works by F. N. Robinson (for details of this
and other editions see page 85). Since the systems of line numbering
vary in most modern editions, the following table of equivalent lines
may be useful for reference:

	Coghill and Tolkien	Havely	Spearing	Robinson; Cawley
General Prologue Portrait	I, 669–714	1–46	I, 671–716	I, 669–714
Headlink	1–40	1–40	1–42	VI, 287–328
Pardoner's Prologue	41–174	41–174	43–176	VI, 329–462
Pardoner's Tale	175–615	175–615	177–617	VI, 463–903
Epilogue	616–80	616–80	618–82	VI, 904–68

1 CHAUCER'S LIFE AND WORKS

1.1 CHAUCER'S LIFE

The year of Chaucer's birth is not known for certain, but it was probably not long after 1340, for in 1386 he described himself as aged 'forty years old and more'. His mother was probably called Agnes, and his father was John Chaucer, a prosperous London wine merchant, whose social aspirations led him to attend occasionally upon King Edward III.

A child of young Geoffrey's background would probably have received his basic education first in one of the 'song' schools (so called because they were attached to the cathedrals) and later in a grammar school, where he would have learned Latin and French, the languages in which lessons were normally conducted. However, he is not definitely heard of until 1358, by which time he was a valet in the service of Lionel and Elizabeth, Earl and Countess of Ulster, from whom he received that year a livery of clothing and the sum of two shillings and sixpence 'for necessaries at Christmas'. These years of service were also part of his education, for (as a medieval book of household ordinances tells us) young men like him were expected to seek out the good company of lords and gentlemen and engage

> in talking of chronicles of kings and of other policies [*accomplishments*], or in piping, harping, singing, or martial acts, [and] to help occupy the court and accompany strangers, till the time require of departing.

Chaucer's description of the Squire in the *General Prologue to the Canterbury Tales* is an idealised portrait of a young man at just this stage in his career.

The next fact we know is that in 1359 he was on a military expedition in France, where he was taken prisoner. King Edward paid £16, a large sum in those days, towards his ransom; we do not know if this was the full amount, but, whatever the case, the sum suggests that Chaucer was already a person of importance, for much smaller sums were paid for other valets of the court. Chaucer acted as a courier in the peace negotiations of 1360, for which he received nine shillings from Prince Lionel.

In the ensuing six years nothing is heard of him at all. One theory is that he was studying law at one of the Inns of Court in London, another that he was in Ireland with Prince Lionel. It was probably in this period, about 1366, that he married Philippa Roet, a lady-in-waiting to the queen. Her sister, Katherine, was later married to John of Gaunt, son of Edward III and one of the greatest nobles of his day, and as a result Chaucer actually became related to the royal family. By his marriage Chaucer seems to have had at least three children – Elizabeth, Thomas, and the 'little Lewis' for whom he translated the scientific *Treatise on the Astrolabe*, though some say (judging from the extreme generosity of John of Gaunt to both Philippa and Geoffrey Chaucer) that Elizabeth and Thomas may have been the illegitimate children of Gaunt himself. Philippa was Chaucer's wife for over twenty years, until her death in 1387, about the time when he was embarking on *The Canterbury Tales*.

In the years 1366–98 Chaucer was engaged in extensive travels abroad in the service of the king. Many of the details are obscure, and some of the journeys were secret, concerning perhaps delicate matters of diplomacy or trade. The countries he visited include Spain (1366), France (1368), 'parts beyond the sea' (1370), Italy (1372–3), some unspecified place or places 'in secret negotiations for the king' (1376–81), Italy again (1378), and France again (1387). Presumably he had a flair for foreign languages, including by this time Italian. The visits to France and Italy were to have a profound effect on his writings, for they brought him into contact with important men of letters whose new and exciting ideas he incorporated and adapted in his own works.

By 1367 Chaucer seems to have left the service of Prince Lionel and become an esquire of the royal household. In that year he received from the king a pension of twenty marks (approximately £13) for life, to which in 1374 was added an award of a daily pitcher of wine. That same year he was given rent-free accommodation in a house over Aldgate, one of the gates of the city of London, which he occupied for the next twelve years. This year also saw the first of a number of public and professional appointments when he became

Controller of Customs and Subsidy of Wools, Skins and Hides in the Port of London; for this important job the salary was £10, to which was added an annual bonus of ten marks; but he probably received more than this in fees and 'perks', such as the sum of over £71, the fine of a merchant caught trying illegally to export wool, which was given over to him in 1376. Another appointment in 1375–6 was to the lucrative guardianship of two young heirs in Kent; another in 1382 was to a Controllership of Petty Customs on Wines and other Goods; and another in 1385–9 was to the office of Justice of the Peace for Kent. This last appointment shows that he must have moved from London to Kent, probably to Greenwich, because only residents were eligible to become Justices of the Peace. Obviously he was making a great success of his public career, and in 1386 he was elected as one of the two Knights of the Shire to represent Kent in Parliament.

During the time of Chaucer's Controllership an obscure incident took place which has puzzled his biographers ever since the facts were discovered. In 1380 a woman named Cecily Champain, daughter of a baker, released him from a charge of *raptus*. In fourteenth-century law the term could refer to a number of crimes, from physical rape to abduction; Chaucer's own father had been abducted as a child in an attempt to force him into an unwished-for marriage, and Geoffrey himself served in 1387 on a commission to investigate the alleged *raptus* of a Kentish heiress. In the case of Cecily Champain the known facts are simply insufficient to show clearly the nature of the alleged crime or Chaucer's supposed part in the affair, whether as a principal or an accomplice of those accused with him. The fact that the charge against him was withdrawn may argue for his complete innocence. All the same, the matter casts a faint shadow of suspicion, however unfairly, over Chaucer's otherwise unblemished reputation.

Chaucer retired from his duties as Controller of Customs in 1386. This change may have been connected with a decline in the influence of his political friends and supporters at court. Richard II, grandson of Edward III, had become king in 1377 at the age of ten, and Chaucer's Controllership and pensions had at that time been reaffirmed. But in the mid-1380s John of Gaunt's influence over the young king began to diminish as his brother Thomas, Duke of Gloucester, rose to power. These years saw Chaucer sued for debt (1388), and it could be that the change in political circumstances is mirrored in the change in his own fortunes. However, the situation is far from clear, and Chaucer's financial ups and downs seem to have continued, whatever the reason, until the very end of his life.

In 1389 Chaucer was appointed Clerk of the King's Works, the official in charge of royal buildings, and in 1390 was included in a royal commission on the mundane-sounding subject of walls and ditches. During this period he was attacked and robbed several times of large sums of money belonging to the Works. He was absolved of the responsibility to repay the stolen money, but these unpleasant experiences may have induced him to give up the task before two years had elapsed. He moved straight to a job as deputy forester for the royal forest of North Petherton in Somerset; his duties were to oversee the rangers and gamekeepers – men like the Yeoman on the Canterbury pilgrimage. This was more successful, and he seems to have continued in this office for most of the remaining years of his life.

Chaucer continued to receive grants and pensions from Richard II until the latter's deposition in 1399. The new king, Henry IV, was already acquainted with Chaucer, and in 1396 had given him a fine gown trimmed with fur. Upon his accession he immediately reconfirmed Chaucer's annual pension of £20 granted in 1394, and, in fact, increased it with an annuity of twenty marks; and he did not forget the annual butt of wine which had been Chaucer's since 1397. All the signs are that Chaucer at the very end of his life, as in most of his adult years, was a valued and respected royal servant.

On Christmas Eve 1399 Chaucer took out a lease for 53 years of a house in the garden of the Lady Chapel of Westminster Abbey in London. But his residence there could only have been brief, for within a year, on 25 October 1400, he was dead, his age probably a little short of sixty. He was buried in the Abbey, and occupies an honoured place in what has since become known as Poets' Corner.

These brief facts tell us quite a lot about Chaucer's public life but almost nothing about his character and personality, for which his works themselves are the primary source of information. The historical records show that he was both civil servant and courtier. In the former capacity he would have met a wide variety of people, for most of the jobs were not sinecures; and in the latter he would have been close to men of rank, including royalty, though his own middle-class background would have necessitated a degree of modesty, which is something he often affects in his writings. Although none of the payments to him is specifically said to be for literary services, we may reasonably conjecture that this was so. One of his last works is a short begging poem, *The Complaint of Chaucer to his Purse*, which is addressed to Henry IV; judging from the annuity of forty marks he received in October 1399, the poem did not fall on deaf ears.

1.2 CHAUCER'S MAIN WORKS

The earliest influences on Chaucer's style of writing and choice of subjects were French. Possibly one of his first undertakings was a translation of the long French allegorical poem *Le Roman de la Rose*, in which a lover dreams that he is searching for a rose (symbolic of his lady) in a beautiful walled garden peopled by personified abstractions such as Idleness and Chastity; however, Chaucer's part in the authorship of the version which survives is not certain. Another early work is *The Book of the Duchess*, also a dream poem, which is said to have been composed as an elegy to Blanche (died 1369), first wife of John of Gaunt. Yet another dream poem is *The House of Fame*, in which Chaucer imagines himself carried by an eagle to a palace dedicated to famous people of old; the poem, which is unfinished and breaks off inconsequentially, shows the beginnings of the important Italian influence which may have resulted from his travels abroad. *The Parliament of Fowls* is yet another dream poem; in it the poet imagines himself to be in a beautiful garden on St Valentine's Day, where he witnesses a gathering of birds at which they all choose their partners for the coming year. *Troilus and Criseyde* is the longest poem which Chaucer completed, and tells a tragic love story set in ancient Troy. Both this and the *Parliament* are strongly influenced by Italian writers such as Boccaccio, Dante and Petrarch, as well as by the famous Latin work *The Consolation of Philosophy* of the philosopher Boethius (c. 480–c. 524 A.D.), of which Chaucer made a prose translation, probably around 1380. Next in sequence is another work never completed, *The Legend of Good Women*; in it Chaucer pretends to be acting under the instructions of the God of Love to tell the stories of virtuous women as a penance for having defamed the female sex by having previously told of the faithless Crisyede. Finally comes Chaucer's most famous work, associated predominantly with the period 1387–1400, *The Canterbury Tales*.

1.3 THE CANTERBURY TALES

This was a grand design which was never completed. In the *General Prologue* a fictional framework is set up in which Chaucer describes himself meeting a party of pilgrims at the Tabard Inn in Southwark, London, from where they were shortly to set off on a journey to the shrine of St. Thomas Becket in Canterbury. The Host of the Tabard, Harry Bailly, proposes a plan to keep them amused. Each pilgrim shall tell two tales on the outward journey and two on the return, and the teller of the best tale shall be rewarded by a supper paid for by all the others. This is the only point at which the ambitious four-tale scheme is mentioned; the pilgrims are usually simply told that they have to tell a tale, though once or twice mention is casually made of 'a tale or two' or 'tales two or three'. The Host's scheme for four tales each, then, may have been a hopeful plan from which Chaucer later departed, or alternatively a late idea which he failed to develop by returning to and revising the parts he had already written. At all events, instead of the one hundred and twenty tales which the 'nyne and twenty' pilgrims plus Chaucer himself should rightly have told (according to the Host), only twenty-four have actually come down to us, including two from Chaucer and one from a Canon's Yeoman who joins the party at a later point.

To compound the difficulty, *The Canterbury Tales* survives only in a series of fragments, which seem not to have been arranged by Chaucer in any particular order. These can be grouped into approximately ten sections on the evidence of the linking passages which occur in some places and which describe reactions to the tale just told and give Harry Bailly's invitation to the teller of the next. There is no problem about how the work was meant to start, for the section known as Fragment I contains the *General Prologue* and a logically linked sequence of *Knight's Tale, Miller's Tale, Reeve's Tale*, and the unfinished *Cook's Tale*; the end is also known, for in Fragment X the Parson rounds the whole thing off with a sermon, to which most manuscripts append Chaucer's *Retraction*, in which the poet piously revokes all his vain writings, including those of *The Tales of Canterbury*, 'thilke that sownen into synne' ('those that incline towards sin'). The positions of the other fragments are altogether uncertain. Suffice it to say that *The Pardoner's Tale* occurs with only *The Physician's Tale* in that fragment which is traditionally numbered VI. It has a well developed *Headlink*, or introduction (see section 4.3), which shows quite clearly that it was intended to follow *The Physician's Tale*, but there is no indication of what might have come after. It is likely that the Pardoner's perky interruption of *The Wife of Bath's Prologue* (see section 4.2) would not have been thought appropriate after his humiliation at the end of his tale (see section 4.6), so we can deduce that *The Wife of Bath's Prologue* and *Tale* probably were meant to precede the Pardoner's. More than this we cannot say.

The situation may seem simpler if we try to imagine how Chaucer might have gone about things. He would not simply have started on so long and adventurous a project as *The Canterbury Tales* on a particular day and continued with it until his death; the idea would have matured gradually, and he would perhaps have experimented with different approaches and subjects. Two of the surviving tales, those of the Knight and the Second Nun, appear to have been written before the plan for *The Canterbury Tales* came to mind, for Chaucer refers to them elsewhere by different names. Furthermore, he sometimes does not seem to have decided very firmly upon a suitable teller for a tale: the Second Nun oddly refers to herself as an 'unworthy son of Eve', which suggests that her tale may originally have been devised for a man, whereas *The Shipman's Tale*, on similar evidence, seems to have been meant for a female teller. Probably Chaucer would have tried out some of his tales by circulating copies or by having them read aloud at court, but at the time of his death in 1400 the material would have consisted of little more than a bundle of papers or parchment, perhaps in a cupboard or a box under his bed. Before these could be published someone would have had to put them in order, to try to patch together part-written passages, and maybe even to write a few lines here and there to smooth over the gaps. Consequently, it is often dangerous to assume too readily the appropriateness of tale to teller, since the attribution may not represent Chaucer's firm intentions. Happily this does not apply in the case of the Pardoner, whose tale, perhaps more than that of any other, is carefully integrated into the dramatic context of the pilgrimage and is a close reflection of the depraved character who tells it.

For all its unfinished condition, *The Canterbury Tales* is rightly agreed to be Chaucer's finest work. Anyone studying an individual tale cannot afford to neglect the work as a whole, and fortunately there are many translations into modern English. Even for those who have not the opportunity to read the whole work an obvious starting point is the *General Prologue*; it contains portraits of the pilgrims, details of the pilgrimage and the storytelling scheme, and some preliminary remarks by Chaucer (such as his apology in advance for blunt language). Popular tales today are *The Knight's Tale* (a rather long romance of rival lovers set in ancient Athens), *The Miller's Tale, The Reeve's Tale* and *The Merchant's Tale* (all rather bawdy tales of *fabliau* type), *The Wife of Bath's Tale* (interesting like the Pardoner's for its autobiographical prologue and for the lively characterisation of the Wife), and *The Nun's Priest's Tale* (a beast fable with some delightful irony). Excellent as these are, none surpasses *The Pardoner's Tale* in its continuing appeal to scholars and students alike.

2 MEDIEVAL BACKGROUND

2.1 THE DIFFERENCE BETWEEN MEDIEVAL AND MODERN LITERATURE

Medieval literature is different from modern literature and requires a different approach. No one will ever understand Chaucer simply by translating his works into Modern English and subjecting them to present-day techniques of literary analysis. Although Chaucer has a continuing appeal far greater than that of any other medieval English author, if we neglect his background and context we miss the point, we run the risk of making naïve and subjective judgements, we overlook much of what he intended, and we deny ourselves the opportunity to glimpse the richness and relevance which Chaucer's writings would have had for his contemporaries.

2.2 PUBLICATION AND PATRONAGE

An obvious difference concerns the conditions under which a work was composed and made public. A present-day author begins or completes his book and then approaches a publisher; if it is good enough, a contract is arranged and remuneration decided; changes in the content and format may be agreed and there will be several opportunities for the author to check the accuracy of the type-setting as it goes through press. It will have a clear title page, with publication details on the reverse. The end product is therefore a fixed entity which has undergone careful scrutiny and which accurately reflects the aims and intentions of the author.

The situation was very different in Chaucer's time. To begin with, fewer people could write, and the classes of those who could were more restricted. Illiterate authors could and did compose orally, and some if their works which happened to get written down have survived to the present day. An aspiring literate author would usually seek the help of a rich patron and might have to combine the role of writer with some other job, such as that of secretary. The wishes of the patron would affect the type of work composed. Since the church offered a sort of patronage for many medieval writers, as well as providing education for almost all, it is not surprising that the vast majority of medieval works are religious. The author might then arrange for a particularly lavish copy of his work to be made specifically for the patron; presentation copies of such books survive, some with a frontispiece depicting the author on his knee handing over the book.

Chaucer enjoyed the patronage of three successive kings: Edward III, Richard II, and (briefly) Henry IV. Since his writings were popular during his lifetime and his poetic output was large, he would have been engaged in a constant struggle to have his works accurately set down. A short poem of his addressed to Adam 'his owne scriveyn' ('his own scribe') wishes upon him a scabby disease under his long hair unless he transcribes more accurately. Chaucer complains that he often has to go over the copies Adam has made, correcting and scraping the mistakes from the parchment, and that all this trouble is the result of Adam's negligence and haste.

Once a composition was presented it could be put into circulation, and thereafter the author had virtually no control. All works had to be copied by hand, and transcribers naturally made mistakes. They also made deliberate, and sometimes drastic, abridgement, or modernised the language, or changed words to confirm to a dialect other than that of the original. In poetry this sometimes had a devastating effect on the rhyme and metre, and those poems which are extant in only a single corrupt copy are usually beyond salvation. *The Canterbury Tales* was a popular work and survives in an exceptionally large number of manuscripts (over eighty), the earliest dating from soon after Chaucer's death. But some of these are poor copies and some merely fragments. Even with so many manuscripts there are many editorial difficulties, and the present-day printed version can only represent what in the editor's opinion is most likely to reflect Chaucer's intentions. Different editions may therefore contain differences of text one from another; even the punctuation, which is inserted by the editor (since medieval punctuation is usually haphazard and unhelpful), may significantly affect the meaning.

It is often claimed that Chaucer published his works by reading them aloud at court; a fifteenth-century picture of him reading his *Troilus and Criseyde* at the court of Richard II is sometimes cited as evidence. While this may at times have happened, it is also known that manuscripts were circulated for a reading public, as may have been the case with stories from *The Canterbury Tales*. We cannot say for certain whether Chaucer intended his *Pardoner's Tale* to appeal to the ear, but without doubt its sermon-like qualities and rich rhetoric lend an exceptional power to the poem when it is read aloud. exceptional power to the poem when it is read aloud.

2.3 THE CONTENT OF ENGLISH WRITINGS IN CHAUCER'S TIME

From the time of the Norman Conquest of England in 1066 until Chaucer's own time in the fourteenth century, English did not have much prestige as a literary language. French, initially the language of the ruling classes in England, was for a long time considered by rich patrons to be much more acceptable, but even French was overshadowed by the international language of learning and literature, Latin. All this is reflected in the relative numbers of manuscripts which survive, Latin manuscripts being by far the most numerous. As far as we know, Chaucer did not compose in French or Latin, though some contemporary English poets did, such as his friend John Gower, who wrote major poems in all three languages.

Chaucer, Gower, William Langland and the so-called *Gawain* poet are the names most closely associated with the sudden flowering of English literature which took place in the second half of the fourteenth century. Gower's main English work, like Chaucer's, is a collection of tales brought within a unifying frame; although called *Confessio Amantis*, that is, *The Confessions of a Lover*, this has a serious moral purpose, for the tales are selected to exemplify sin and how best to avoid it. Chaucer and Gower together represent the courtly style in English poetry, one of the characteristics of which is the use of lines which rhyme, as in much of the verse from between their time and the present day. Conversely Langland and the *Gawain* poet are noted for their preference for alliterative verse, in which the lines are arranged so that some of the most important words form patterns which begin with the same sound, as in the line:

Sheer sheds the rain in showers full warm.

This style of poetry, though it is often sophisticated in its own way, was considered more of a provincial accomplishment. Langland's only known work is called *Piers Plowman*, an enigmatic dream-vision in which the author explores through allegory the fundamental problems which beset the honest Christian who desires to lead a good life. The author of *Sir Gawain and the Green Knight* is not known by name, but his poem is an alliterative masterpiece which treats courtly and moral concern in the context of a brilliantly-told romance; the three other poems in the same, unique, manuscript, *Pearl*, *Patience* and *Purity*, are probably by the same poet.

A whole range of lesser poems has survived from medieval England. For instance, there are popular romances, mostly translated or adapted from French, telling exciting stories about chivalry and love, utilising stock situations and characters; there are stories of the lives of saints, which owed much of their popularity to their descriptions of spectacular miracles, as well as often to gory details of martyrdom; there are animal fables, which highlight folly by exploring the human condition in a non-human context; there are *fabliaux*, verse tales of sexual impropriety in which an elaborately-planned deception goes hilariously wrong; there are satirical poems dealing with contemporary conditions, such as politics, the follies of fashion or the abuses of the friars; and there are debate poems, in which conflicting views are put forth by such opposites as 'Body and Soul' or 'Owl and Nightingale'. In addition there are shorter poems by various authors, secular and religious, which today go under the name of Middle English Lyrics; some of these were once accompanied by music, and in a few cases the musical notation survives; the subjects include dance songs, praise for beautiful ladies, lovers' complaints, songs welcoming the spring, drinking songs, bawdy songs, reflections on Christ's sufferings, laments of the Blessed Virgin at the cross, and sober thoughts on death and the instability of worldly riches and pleasures.

Verse was sometimes preferred to prose even for practical works such as chronicles, catechisms, treatises on hunting, weather predictions and even gardening books. English prose, however, had long been used for sermons and certain other categories of religious work, and in Chaucer's day it was increasing in importance in many spheres, especially that of translation. The greatest of all fourteenth-century translations into English is the Wycliffite Bible, which was at the heart of a fierce debate about the desirability of translating the scriptures into the vernacular. The great proponent of translation was John Wyclif, who argued that the established church wished to keep the word of God from the people in order to hide its many abuses. Wyclif was the spearhead of the project to translate the Bible into English prose, but this remarkable ambition was achieved not by him alone but through a team of translators and revisers. In Chaucer's day the established church still thought that it was dangerous and heretical to study the Bible in English, and Wycliffites (often branded 'Lollards') had to meet and worship in secret.

Finally there is the drama, of which the major surviving varieties are the Mystery Plays, verse dramatisations of Biblical history from the Creation to Doomsday as performed in towns throughout the country, and the Morality Plays, treatments in verse of the subject of sin and salvation, focusing upon a representative human being ('Everyman' or 'Mankind') who is assailed by various personifications of vice but saved eventually by God's mercy.

It is a tribute to Chaucer's versatility that *The Canterbury Tales* exemplifies a number of these genres. For example *The Nun's Priest's Tale* is an animal fable, *The Miller's Tale* and *The Reeve's Tale* are both typical of the *fabliau, The Parson's Tale* is a sermon and *The Knight's Tale* a courtly romance. Chaucer even depicts himself, 'Chaucer the Canterbury pilgrim', as telling the romance of *Sir Topas*; the irony is that it turns out to be such a caricature of the low, 'popular' romance that the other pilgrims cannot bear to hear the tale through to its finish, and Chaucer is shouted down. It is one of his most endearing characteristics that he was able to make fun of himself.

2.4 CHAUCER'S ENGLAND

The age in which Chaucer lived, the second half of the fourteenth century, was a time of huge social and political change. It was inaugurated by a devastating plague, the Black Death of 1348–9, which killed perhaps between a third and a half of the total population of England, and it was brought to an end by the enforced abdication of Richard II in 1399 and his death the following year under mysterious circumstances, possibly at the instigation of the new king, Henry IV.

When Chaucer was born, around the year 1340, Edward III was on the throne of England. An outstanding soldier, instigator of the so-called Hundred Years' War, victor over the Scots and French (most famously at Crécy in 1346), his early reign promised much which was not fulfilled. In his later years the war with France seemed just as far from resolution as when it began, and at home court life was overshadowed by the dominance of his unpopular mistress, Alice Perrers. When Edward died in 1377 he was succeeded by his young grandson, Richard II, son of the Black Prince. During Richard's minority the principal power at court was John of Gaunt, under whose patronage Chaucer was advanced in social position; but John's brother, Thomas of Gloucester, came to power in 1386, and thereafter Chaucer was less secure. Richard's reign was one of even greater contrast between early promise and eventual disappointment. His court was the centre of a renaissance in the arts and literature, in which Chaucer played no small part. Richard was also popular with the ordinary people, so it is ironic that the greatest upheaval of the century occurred in his reign, in the form of the Peasants' Revolt of 1381.

The roots of this lay in the Black Death and the recurrences of plague in 1361 and 1369. The huge mortality led to a great shortage of agricultural labour, and working men found that they were suddenly in a position to demand higher wages. Large numbers left the jobs in which their families had toiled for generations and went in search of the highest bidder for their services. In an attempt to settle the resulting unrest a Statute of Labourers was enacted in 1351, to fix the price of labour at the rate which had been in force before the plague; able-bodied men were not allowed to refuse any work which was offered them, and it was as illegal to offer more than the standard wage as it was to demand it. For a while the statute held down prices, but the peasantry could scarcely smother its discontent, which was made worse by the imposition of unpopular taxes. In 1381 large numbers of labourers marched on London from Kent and Essex. Under their leader Wat Tyler they vented their anger against a number of figures whom they considered representative of the establishment, especially John of Gaunt, who was forced to escape to Scotland. Richard's personal intervention finally placated the rebels, but not before the threat to London had thoroughly frightened all established residents, Chaucer among them.

It was Chaucer's London which must have provided the inspiration for many of the characters who take part in the famous Canterbury pilgrimage, though we need not go so far as to suppose that he necessarily had individual models in mind or even that he sought to be realistic in his portrayals of them. It is estimated that at this time London had a population of about forty thousand living in the square mile within its walls. It was the greatest commercial centre in England. The flourishing guilds, or craft and trade fraternities, controlled much of the economic, social and artistic life of the city, while the royal court would have been another attraction to people with flair and talent. Chaucer's world was so different from our own that it requires great expertise to interpret correctly even the most ordinary facts, or else a great effort of the imagination – or both. Chaucer's biographer John Gardner is good at putting the two together, and in passages like the following probably comes close to evoking the spirit of the times:

> England's great poet of gentleness and compassion walked every day in a city where the fly-bitten, bird-scarred corpses of hanged criminals – men and women, even children – draped their shadows across the crowded public square. If the crime was political, the corpse was tarred to prevent its decaying before the achievement of the full measure of its shame. As Chaucer strolled across London Bridge, making up intricate ballades in his head, counting beats on his fingers, he could see, if he looked up, the staked heads of wrongdoers hurried away by earnest Christians to their presumed eternal torment. With our modern sensibilities we would certainly object and perhaps interfere – as Chaucer never did – and for the attempt to undermine the king's peace, not to mention God's, our severed heads would go up on the stakes beside those others.

It is difficult to imagine the outdoor plays, tournaments, spectacles, saints' day festivals and other traditional events which were part of ordinary life and which helped colour Chaucer's view of the world. It was a fast-changing, smelly, disease-ridden, dangerous and authoritarian world, but it was also exciting, productive and full of opportunities for a lucky few. We have reason to be thankful that Chaucer was among them.

2.5 THE INTELLECTUAL BACKGROUND

The medieval understanding of history, science and theology – in fact, every thought and attitude of mind – was affected by a belief in a single, complex and harmonious model of the universe, which placed God at the top and every creature and object in its proper place. Consequently, the heavens, the natural world, social institutions, the human body, and even inanimate objects were thought to be logically and interdependently organised, and any departure from the natural order was thought to cause a *frisson* of shock waves throughout the system.

Following a concept of the universe devised by the second-century Egyptian astronomer Ptolemy, Chaucer and his contemporaries believed that the earth was a sphere (not flat, as is commonly claimed) at the centre of nine concentric transparent 'spheres', or 'heavens'; the first seven each contained one of the planets and the eighth was set with the 'fixed stars'; the ninth was the 'prime mover', an invisible sphere which was the source of all motion in the others. This harmonious movement produced a divine music, 'the music of the spheres', which was more sublime than the most exquisite music made by man. All other things within this universe were beautifully organised into a hierarchical 'chain of being', from God and the angels to humans, beasts, plants and mere objects. Within each category there were sub-categories, such as the ranks of human society, and in the physical world the 'elements', air, fire, water and earth, corresponding to the 'humours' of blood, choler, phlegm and melancholy, which by their proportions in any individual's body determined that person's particular temperament, or 'complexion'. Medieval thinkers and writers were organisers, categorisers and lovers of system, and C. S. Lewis (writing in *The Discarded Image* in 1964) suspected that of all modern inventions they would most have admired the card index.

It is less important to remember the details of the system than to grasp how profoundly it affected medieval attitudes and made them different from our own. Insight was not gained by observation and hypothesis, as it had been by the Greeks. It was felt that the truth had already been revealed and was there to be discovered in the writings of former ages. Consequently medieval culture was overwhelmingly dependent on books, even though fewer people then could read. Every writer tried to base his work upon an earlier writer – preferably a Latin one, since they had the most status. Originality, in the sense of new plots and themes, was not highly prized. Hence Chaucer usually reworked established stories, and disguised new material even to the extent of inventing an authority, such as the 'Lollius' whom he claims to be following in writing *Troilus and Criseyde*. This does not make his writings dull or derivative (it has, in fact, been said that Chaucer was never more original than when borrowing); but it does make them different from what we are used to, and that is why the background deserves a little thought.

2.6 THE CHURCH

In this age of authorities there was no greater authority than the Roman Catholic Church. The control which it exercised over individuals and institutions can be traced back to the very introduction of Christianity into England at the end of the sixth century. By the fourteenth century it had grown to become a powerful political, economic, social, educational, moral and, of course, religious force. Large numbers of people were in clerical occupations of some sort, some merely peripheral to the church's work (like Chaucer's Pardoner), others essential (like his Parson). Those who were in orders fell into either of two categories: secular and regular. The secular clergy (from Latin *saecularis*, 'of the world') performed the functions of present-day clergymen in caring for people's souls; Chaucer's Parson is again an example. The regular clergy (from Latin *regularis*, 'governed by a rule') were those who had taken vows of communal life, such as Chaucer's Monk and Prioress. For many centuries the church had controlled all levels of the country's education system, and even in Chaucer's day, when the situation was changing, it was still often assumed that the purpose of an education was to prepare a man or woman for religious life. The church owned vast estates and capital, and could demand taxes and dues of its own. It was influential at court, in parliament, and in all levels of the civil service. It provided care for the sick and poor. It had its own courts, at which those offenders claiming 'benefit of clergy' were tried according to canon law (which was reckoned to be more lenient than civil law). It enforced regular weekly attendance at church, where the services were conducted in Latin and the scriptures expounded from the pulpit. Through its priests it administered the sacraments, such as Baptism, Communion, Marriage, Penance and the Last Rites to the dying, all of which were tremendously important to a society of believers. In short, its influence in every sphere of life can hardly be overestimated. Of course, there were parts of this vast organisation which were corrupt, and Chaucer recognised this and exposed many of the abuses in *The Canterbury Tales*. But this does not undermine the fact that the original audience of *The Pardoner's Tale* would have comprised men and women who knew a good sermon from a bad who understood the church's teaching on sin, who were respectful of the authority of the Pope, and who were terrified of the torments of hell – attitudes which most of us, from our position of 'enlightenment', can only with some labour seek to reconstruct.

3 CHAUCER'S LANGUAGE

3.1 MIDDLE ENGLISH

All living languages are in a constant state of change, so it is hardly surprising that Chaucer's English, now six hundred years old, is rather different from our own. Sometimes the rate of change in language speeds up under the influence of outside events, and two such times of exceptional change are recognised in the history of English, resulting in three periods, known as Old English (c. 700 to c. 1150), Middle English (c. 1150 to c. 1500), and Modern English (c. 1500 to the present). It was the overthrow of the Anglo-Saxons by the Normans which brought about the change from Old to Middle English. The factors which led to the end of Middle English are less easy to summarise, but include social change, increased communication, and the spread of printing. There were also changes at this time to which no definite cause can be ascribed; one such was the sound change known as the Great Vowel Shift, whereby all the long vowels of Middle English, which were formerly pronounced rather like vowels of French or Italian, began to be 'raised', that is, pronounced with the tongue in a much higher position in the mouth. This was a very far-reaching change and accounts more than anything for the difference in sound between Chaucer's English and our own. And in addition general tendencies towards change in English have continued to take place from Chaucer's time to the present, such as the ongoing weakening and loss of unstressed syllables which has resulted in the weakening and loss of many of the old inflexional endings (those grammatically-significant terminations of words, such as *-en* and *-eth*, which have been steadily disappearing right up to the present day).

Middle English literature is typified by the use of a range of regional dialects. For most of the period writers from, say, the west country wrote unselfconsciously in a west country dialect, those from Kent wrote in Kentish, and so on. The reason for this is that there was no such sense of a 'standard' as there is in Modern English. Standard English of today is the English which is typically used in the media, in business and the civil service, and in the teaching of the language throughout the world; though it developed from a regional dialect it has lost its regional characteristics. Such a thing in Chaucer's day did not exist, but the situation was beginning to change, and in the later fourteenth century a written standard based on the dialect of London was beginning to emerge which in the course of time grew into the written and spoken standard throughout the country. As London grew more important economically, politically and socially, and particularly with the influx into the capital of large numbers of people from the rich and populous east midlands, London English began to assume a status which other dialects did not have. Chaucer himself helped to give prestige to London English, as did other writers such as Wyclif and Langland, and later Caxton and Malory, who were born in other parts of England but chose to use the emerging standard of London in their works. When Caxton, England's first printer, set up his press in Westminster in 1476, he had difficulty in deciding which variety of English to use in his publications. In the prologue to his translation of the *Aeneid* of Virgil, 1490, he tells an anecdote about a merchant called Sheffield from the north of England, who, on a visit to the London region, asked his landlady for *eggys* to eat. The woman replied that she could not speak French, and the merchant was angry, for neither could he. Then someone explained that what he wanted was *eyren*, and the woman understood him perfectly, because this was the normal form of the word in her dialect. Caxton asks in exasperation:

Loo, what sholde a man in thyse dayes now wryte, 'eggys' or 'eyrn'? Certaynly it is harde to playse euery man, because of dyversyte and chaunge of language.

The fact that he and other early printers chose the English of London was a consideration in its rise in importance. As a consequence Chaucer's English, because it is the ancestor of modern Standard English, seems much less strange to present-day readers than contemporary writings in other dialects, such as the works of the *Gawain* poet or many of the Middle English Lyrics.

It would be wrong, of course, to suppose that the language of Chaucer's poetry is closely comparable to that which was spoken by ordinary people. Chaucer was a court poet and his style is therefore the courtly style. One of the signs of this is his choice of vocabulary, for even a casual reader will notice a preponderance of words derived from French, and ultimately from Latin – words such as *auctoritee, habitacioun, mesurable, predicacioun, superfluytee*, and others much more humble such as *clerk, delit, maladye, pardoun* and *visage*; these reflect his preference for French literary models and the fact that French was still frequently spoken at court. Chaucer also avoided the provincial alliterative style of poetry, preferring instead the more fashionable end-rhyme. He used a variety of verse forms, but the most common in *The Canterbury Tales*, and the form which is used in all parts involving the Pardoner, is the rhyming couplet in lines of ten syllables ('pentameters'), lines which have the same basic rhythm as those of Shakespeare's blank verse. The rhythm admits considerable variety, and Chaucer achieves some of his most effective verse by at times introducing the varied rhythms of ordinary speech into the more metrically regular pattern which is the norm.

3.2 READING CHAUCER

Students new to Chaucer are likely to find his language difficult, and it may be a natural reaction to treat him almost as if he were the writer of a foreign language, and to work slowly through his poems, translating virtually word-for-word with the aid of a glossary. Although notice must indeed be taken of the precise meanings of words, it is a mistake to lose oneself like this in the process of translating. It is difficult to imagine how anyone toiling away in this manner can ever hope to acquire an enjoyment of the 'feel' of the language, or even to sense the qualities of the poetry. Two particular lines of approach may be helpful. One is to read as much Chaucer as possible, naturally in translation at first; the effect will be to introduce his literary environment, his ideas and his interests, all of which will immeasurably reduce the initial strangeness, even perhaps of the language, for a translation will tend to eradicate the problem of mere spelling differences and emphasise the fundamental similarities between Middle and Modern English.

The second approach is to read Chaucer (aloud if circumstances permit) with regard for the original pronunciation, for there is no better way to acquire an intuitive understanding of him. Almost every edition of his poems contains a table of Middle English sounds, but these are very difficult to apply without guidance. A much better way is to learn by imitation, and here an informed teacher or a recording is likely to be of most help (for the latter see pp. 86–7). It is, of course, reasonable to ask how we can know today what Chaucer's English sounded like. The answer is that we cannot know for certain, but that it can be reconstructed in a form which would probably have been comprehensible to listeners of the time. The evidence is drawn from changes in English which have occurred since the fifteenth century (when grammarians first began to describe the sounds of English); from comparison with other languages, especially French; from a careful analysis of spelling, which at that time was more closely representative of the actual sounds than is the case today; and from considerations of rhyme and rhythm. If all these are taken into consideration it is possible to achieve a pronunciation which is both acceptable on historical principles and also enables Chaucer to be read aloud in a way which makes good sense.

Though it may seem rather specific in the present context, it is worth mentioning briefly three considerations which may be a cause of particular difficulty; spelling, accent and the pronunciation of final -*e*.

Spelling is more of an apparent problem than a real one. The spelling system encountered in editions is a slightly modernised form of the spelling of the fifteenth-century manuscripts in which Chaucer's writings are preserved. Since spelling was not so rigidly fixed as today, and since more variation was permissible in the pronunciation of words (especially in rhyme), one sometimes finds different spellings of the same word (for example *hand/hond, pardoner/pardoneer*. Spelling should be taken more at face value than today, so in *nyghte* the *gh* is not silent but pronounced (like the *ch* in Scottish 'loch'). Similarly the doubling of a vowel indicates length (for example *goode*, with the vowel sound of Modern English 'note'). Often *y* is used where we would now use *i* (for example *drynke, synne*). Understanding of such matters comes quickly with practice.

On the question of accent, the rhymes show that Chaucer's English was different from Modern English; the fact that *heer* rhymes with *pardoneer* shows that in words of more than one syllable the final one must sometimes have been accentuated. The difference is particularly apparent in two-syllable words borrowed from French, for where we accentuate the first syllable Chaucer accentuated the second (for example *page* rhyming with *village*). The ending -*ioun* was pronounced as two syllables with the accent on the second; thus *toun* rhymes with *conclusioun*.

The third matter, that of final -*e*, is much more complex, and scholars are still not agreed as to where and when it should be pronounced. In Modern English in such words as 'home' and 'save' it is silent and in most ordinary speech in Chaucer's day it had probably ceased to be sounded. Chaucer seems to have taken advantage of the fluid situation, so that sometimes he retains the pronunication of final -e (for example *Rome*, rhyming with *to me*), and sometimes he obviously intends it to be dropped. The final syllables in words like *lustes* and *shryned* were also pronounced. Where this was so the *e* was unaccented and had the sound of the first syllable in the modern word 'about'.

The golden rule is to pronounce each line of verse with regard to the sense and with a reasonable rhythm, whereupon difficulties of spelling, accent of final -e will be quickly overcome.

3.3 DIFFICULT OR CONFUSABLE WORDS

Some of Chaucer's words are difficult because they have no exact modern equivalent while others are confusing because they have the appearance of modern words but meanings which are rather different. Wider reading of Chaucer helps one become familiar with such words, but it may be useful to have some of the difficulties concerning the Pardoner pinpointed in the order in which they occur. In the list below, the modern form of the word is given in square brackets; this is in most cases *not* the meaning to be understood. Fuller definitions, with examples and dates as to when particular meanings were current, are given in the multi-volume *Complete Oxford English Dictionary*, which is a marvellous research tool for anyone thinking of going on to a higher level of study of Chaucer.

The portrait in the *General Prologue*
gentil [gentle], 671, fine, noble (certainly not 'gentle'). A difficult
    word to translate simply, and often used ironically.
stif [stiff], 673, strong (possibly also 'stiff'; see *burdoun* below)
burdoun [burden], 673, bass accompaniment in singing. There is a
    serious possibility that this also had an obscene meaning, with *stif*
    burdoun reflecting the Summoner's role in a homosexual relation-
    ship.
jolitee [jolity], 680, affectation (though other meanings are
    possible)
walet [wallet], 681, 686, bag (larger than a modern wallet)
hym thoughte [think], 682, it seemed to him (an impersonal
    construction)
dischevelee [dishevelled], 683, with hair unbound, not necessarily
    untidily
smal [small], 688, high-pitched
smothe [smooth], 676, smoothly (an adverb)
late [late], 690, recently (an adverb)

person [parson[, 702 etc, parish priest, parson
upon lond [upon land], 702, in a rural (upland) place
koude [can[, 709 etc, knew how to
storie [story], 709, passage from the scriptures or a saint's life etc (cf. modern 'history')

The Headlink
japes [jape], 319, jokes, amusing anecdotes
anon [anon], 319, 323, immediately
wol [will], 322, wish
gentils [gentle], 323, people of rank and quality (more than common but less than noble)
gonne [begin], 323. Here an auxiliary verb indicating past tense; *gonne to crye* therefore means 'cried'.
wit [wit], 326, piece of wisdom
honeste [honest], 328, respectable

The Pardoner's Prologue
kan [can], 332 etc, know (cf. *General Prologue, koude*)
theme [theme], 333, 425, text (of a sermon)
oon [one], 333, the same
pronounce [pronounce], 335, announce
clerk [clerk], 339, 391, cleric, scholar, any man in holy or minor orders (here used unspecifically)
tales [tale], 341, information, discourse, that which is to be said
devocioun [devotion], 346, religious feeling
worm [worm], 355, serpent, snake, worm or creeping creature
his [his], 356, its (the regular possessive form of *it*, 357)
hool [whole], 357, 359, healed
good-man [goodman], 361, householder, smallholder
oweth [owe], 361, owns
fastynge [fasting], 363, before having eaten
stoor [store], 365, livestock
rage [rage], 367, frenzy
taken [take], 371, taken (as lovers)
offre [offer], 376 etc, make an offering (of money or goods)
wonne [win], 389 etc, earned, acquired
lewed [lewd], 392, 437, ignorant, uneducated
japes [jape], 394, stories or anecdotes told to deceive, tricks (cf. *Headlink*)
bisynesse [business], 399, hard work, diligence
cursednesse [cursedness], 400, wickedness
free [free], 401, generous

namely [namely], 402, especially

nat but [not but, nobbut], 403, merely

nothyng [nothing], 404, not at all

plesance [pleasance], 409, causing of pleasure

veyne [vain], 411, empty, worthless. 'Vainglory' is unwarranted pride.

debate [debate], 412, contend, confront directly

smerte [smart], 413, painfully (an adverb)

trespased [trespass], 416, done harm, done wrong

propre [proper], 417, own

quyte [quit], 420, repay

agayn [again], 427, against

nothyng but for [nothing but for], 433, for no reason except

ensamples [ensample], 435, exemplary tales and instances, *exempla* (see section 6.3)

holde [hold], 438, retain in the memory

wilfully [wilful], 441, of my own free will, by choice

ydelly [idly], 446, unproductively

countrefete [counterfeit], 447, imitate

page [page], 449, servant, person of low rank

sterve [starve], 451, die (not necessarily through lack of food)

joly [jolly], 453, pretty

corny [corny], 456, tasting of corn or malt

hope [hope], 457, expect

vicious [vicious], 459, wicked

The Pardoner's Tale

haunteden [haunt], 464, 547, were regularly involved with

riot [riot], 465, loose living and revelling (see also *riotoures* below)

hasard [hazard], 465 etc, (cf. *hasardour, hasardrye*), gambling, playing the dice game of 'hazard'

superfluytee [superfluity], 471, 528, excess

grisly [grisly], 473, 708, horrifying

totere [tear], 474, tear to pieces (the prefix intensifies the meaning)

smale [small], 478, slim

luxurie [luxury], 484, 897, self-indulgent excess (with connotations of lechery)

unkyndeley [unkindly], 485, 903, unnaturally

shrewe [shrew], 496 etc, wretch, scoundrel

confusion [confusion], 499, utter ruin

boght . . . agayn [buy . . . again], 501, 766, redeemed

aboght [aby, abye], 503, paid for

drede [dread], 507, 561, doubt

deffended [defend], 510, 590, forbidden

oghte us [ought], 512, we ought (an impersonal construction, literally 'it is proper for us')

mesurable [measurable], 515, moderate

tendre [tender], 517, sensitive

deyntee [dainty], 520, delicate, choice, elaborate

mete [meat], 520, 522, food (of all sorts)

kanstow [can, thou], 521, you know how to (a contraction of *kanst* and *thou*)

wombe [womb], 522 etc, belly

corrupcioun [corruption], 535, decay, rottenness

fynde [find], 537, provide for

likerous [likerous, lecherous], 540, sensual

talent [talent], 540, appetite, desire

cure [cure, care], 557, proper manner of behaviour

wit [wit], 559, 778, intelligence

discrecioun [discretion], 559, sound judgement, discernment

conseil [counsel], 561, 819, secret, confidence

subtilly [subtly], 565, 798, cunningly

catel [cattle, chattels], 594, money, property

holde [hold], 598 etc, considered

desolaat [desolate], 598, worthy to be shunned

policye [policy], 600, government

reputacioun [reputation], 602, 626, esteem, good name

agayn [again], 610 etc, back

trouthe [troth], 615 etc, word of honour (not 'truth')

me were levere [lief], 615, I would rather. An impersonal construction, literally 'to me it would be dearer'.

doom [doom], 637, judgement (i.e. where oaths may be sworn soberly, as in a court of law)

in ydel [idle], 642, lightly, 'in vain'

amys [amiss], 642, wrongly

rather [rather], 643, more quickly (i.e. 'sooner' in time)

lete [let], 659, leave, give up

riotoures [rioter], 661 etc. A difficult word for which there is no modern equivalent (cf. 'hooligan', 'reveller', 'debauchee' etc); implies a blend of aggression, dissipation and baseness, with a strong sense of moral disapproval (cf. *riot* above).

knave [knave], 666, servant

redily [readily], 667, quickly

fordronke [drunk], 674, dead drunk (the prefix intensifes the meaning) *privee* [privy], 675, secretive, stealthy

men [man], 675, one (indefinite pronoun)

contree [country], 677, 754, region

avysed [advised], 690, wary

felawes [fellow], 696 etc, comrades

torente [rend], 709, tore to pieces (the prefix intensifes the meaning)

right [right], 712 etc, just, exactly

see [see], 715, watch over

sory [sorry], 717, 877, evil (*With sory grace* is a curse)

forwrapped [wrap], 718, completely muffled up (the prefix intensifies the meaning)

stille [still], 725, unceasingly

cheste [chest], 734, chest of clothes

clowt [clout], 736, cloth (i.e. a shroud)

grace [grace], 737, favour

curteisye [courtesy], 739, good manners, decent behaviour

vileynye [villainy], 740, rudeness

agayns [against], 743, when faced with

hoor [hoar], 743, grey (hair)

where [where], 748, whether

go [go], 748, walk

lightly [lightly], 752, 781, (as) easily

boost [boast], 764, arrogant bluster, swaggering

pleye [play], 778, 827, joke, fool around

myrthe [mirth], 780, happiness, joy (not necessarily 'joviality')

stronge [strong], 789, flagrant, brazen

doon us honge [do . . . hang], 790, cause us to be hanged, have us hanged

wisely [wisely], 792, carefully

slyly [slyly], 792, cleverly

rede [rede], 793, advise, propose

departed [depart], 812 etc, divided

noot [know], 816, do not know (a contraction of negative *ne* and the verb *woot* 'know', cf. 817)

destroyed [destroy], 858, were harming

repaireth [repair], 878, returns

sermone [sermon], 879, talk, speak

suppose [suppose], 889, think

homycide [homicide], 896, murderous

The Epilogue

wyves [wife], 910, women

suffisant [sufficient], 932, competent

in contree [country], 933, across the land

aventures [adventure], 934, accidents, mishaps

seuretee [surety], 937, security, insurance

yfalle [fall], 938, entered by chance

so theech [thee], 947, upon my life (an asseveration). Literally 'as I hope to prosper'; *theech* is a contraction of *thee*, 'prosper', and *ich*, 'I',

breech [breech], 948, breeches (historically plural but here treated as singular, cf.*it*, 949)

fundement [fundament], 950, backside, arse

depeint [depaint], 950, stained, adorned (with excrement)

seintuarie [sanctuary], 953, reliquary, casket for a relic

worthy [worthy], 960, good, deserving respect (in a general sense; cf. *General Prologue, gentil*)

4 THE PARDONER'S PORTRAIT , PROLOGUE AND TALE

4.1 THE PORTRAIT IN THE *GENERAL PROLOGUE*

The Pardoner is the last of the pilgrims to be described in the *General Prologue*. Although Chaucer asks forgiveness for not placing the pilgrims in their proper *degree*, this neglect of him must have carried disparaging connotations to people so mindful of precedence and so rigidly hierarchical in their way of thinking as Chaucer's contemporary public. There may also have been literary and artistic reasons for leaving the Pardoner till last, since he is a boldly drawn character and brings the list to a suitably emphatic end. Chaucer seems to have been particularly interested in him, and, in the Pardoner's own *Prologue* and *Epilogue*, reveals more about him than about any other pilgrim except the Wife of Bath. Clearly, then, the description of the Pardoner in the *General Prologue* ought to be our starting point.

However much the pilgrims give us the impression of their existence as believable individuals, they are primarily types representative of their estates, or positions in society. This is not to deny that some have psychologically credible traits which give them an identity of their own. But Chaucer's audience would have been used to considering outward signs as marks of a person's role or rank in the social hierarchy. For this reason Chaucer was able to rely on preconceived ideas about pardoners, and much of what he tells us merely details the sort of malpractice which many people considered to be part and parcel of that profession. For instance, this passage from the contemporary *Piers Plowman* has a great deal in common with Chaucer's portrait:

> Ther preched a pardoner as he a prest were:
> Broughte forth a bulle with bisshopes seles,
> And seide that himself myghte assoillen hem alle

Of falshede of fastynge, of avowes ybroken.
Lewed men leved hym wel and liked hise wordes,
Comen up knelynge to kissen his bulle.
He bonched hem with his brevet and blered hire eighen,
And raughte with his rageman rynges and broches.
(Prologue, 68–75)

[There was a pardoner, preaching as if he were a priest. He produced a licence sealed with bishops' seals, and claimed to have the power to pardon everyone for failure to keep fasts and for broken vows. The uneducated people believed every word, and were delighted with what he claimed. They came up and knelt to kiss his licence, and he struck them with it and, by means of his roll of parchment, pulled the wool over their eyes and raked in rings and brooches.]

A Pardoner was an official of the church whose duty was to collect charitable offerings for religious purposes on behalf of some ecclesiastical institution. The idea was simple: since the Christian church was keeper of the 'treasury of grace' which had been amassed by Christ and the saints, it might distribute some of that grace through the means of authorised people, who would collect in return some of the worldly riches which were needed for building and equipping churches and hospitals, tending the sick, providing for the destitute, and so on. This became linked with the long-established practice of allowing penitents to atone for their sins by making a money payment instead of undergoing stricter forms of penance, such as fasting or reciting hundreds of prayers. No pardoner was ever entitled to offer a real 'pardon' for a payment of money or goods; real pardons could only be achieved through the sacrament of penance, in which a priest, or someone of similar status, went through carefully defined stages of hearing confession, assuring himself of the genuineness of the repentance, prescribing penance, and pronouncing absolution.

Of course, pardoners often *claimed* more than they should, and Chaucer's is a case in a point. In this instance he is 'of Rouncivale', that is, he is supposed to be acting on behalf of the hospital of the Blessed Mary of Rouncivalle at Charing Cross in London. But we are left in no doubt that the money he collects goes straight into his own pocket. He is exactly the sort about whom the contemporary Pope Boniface IX wrote:

Certain churchmen . . . claim they are sent by us . . . to receive money for us and for the Roman Church, and they go about the country under these pretexts. In this way they announce to the faithful and simple people the real or claimed licences which they have received, and, irreverently abusing those which are real, in pursuit of vile and hateful gain, add to their impudence by claiming false and pretended authorisations of this kind.

There is some evidence that pardoners associated with the hospital of Rouncivalle may have acquired a bad name in all this, for in 1382 (just the time when the idea of *The Canterbury Tales* was maturing) officials of the hospital obtained a writ to bring to justice all those who had claimed to be collecting alms for the hospital but had failed to hand them over. It may even be that Chaucer had a specific scoundrel in mind when he wrote, though no specific evidence has come to light and it would be unwise to take this line of speculation too far.

In the light of the false claims of pardoners, the statement that this one

> streight was comen fro the court of Rome (671)

does not need to be taken at face value. He *might* have been to Rome, of course, and the *vernicle* on his cap is just the sort of badge he might have acquired along the way. But, as we later learn, he is a self-confessed liar and cheat, and the authority he claims surely did not come from the Pope. It is possible either that Chaucer is here adopting the role of naïve pilgrim, neutral observer of things as they might have appeared, or, more likely, that the claim merely echoes the Pardoner's own. The allusion to his wallet, which lay before him in his lap, implies that he is ever ready to practise his scurrilous trade. Moreover, the wallet is

> Bretful of pardoun, comen from Rome al hoot, (687)

the choice of words suggesting that the documents have about as much official status as a bag of hot pies. So there are already plenty of signals that this Pardoner is going to be every bit as bad as the unfavourable stereotype.

This one is friend and *compeer* of the Summoner. A summoner was an officer who served summonses on people to attend the ecclesiastical courts, the sort of person with whom in an ideal world we might expect the Pardoner to have had a professional association, or who in the world of the Canterbury pilgrimage might have been serving a summons on the Pardoner himself, were the one not as corrupt as the other. But the main thing we are told about them is that together they gave a lusty rendering of a secular love song. In giving this information Chaucer is signalling several things. Firstly, the song suggests a worldliness which other information about the Pardoner entirely bears out, since the singing of such songs was often condemned by churchmen as flighty. Secondly, in view of what we have been told about the Summoner's lecherousness and are about to be told about the Pardoner's effeminacy, there is a suggestion of homosexuality, especially if the Summoner's 'stif burdoun', 'deep bass voice', carries the sexual *double entendre* which has been suggested. And thirdly, the singing partnership anticipates the reference to the Pardoner's voice, which is one of a series of outward signs which help to establish his character.

The study of physical features as signs of temperament is known as 'physiognomy'. This was a respected and influential science in medieval times, so the implications of the Pardoner's appearance would have been very obvious. Medieval physiognomy books taught that thin yellow hair is a sign of effeminacy and cunning, glaring, hare-like eyes a sign of gluttony and drunkenness, and a high voice and lack of a beard a sign of lustfulness, impotent fondness for women, and want of honesty. In fact, the signs are so clear that Chaucer goes on to make an uncharacteristically direct statement by way of summary:

> I trowe he were a geldyng or a mare. (691)

Geldyng in Chaucer's day could be used of human eunuchs, not just horses, but *mare* as well as meaning 'woman' carries definite connotations of bestiality, thereby accentuating the implication of moral baseness which medieval people believed was inevitable in a man who lacked virility. Furthermore, the Pardoner has a fondness for fashion which helps to highlight some of these unfortunate features. With his long, thin hair 'he his shuldres overspradde', ironically accentuating one of the very tokens of his depravity. He wore no hood 'for jolitee', that is, 'for affectation' or possibly 'for his own pleasure or fancy'; Chaucer mischievously adds that it was 'trussed up in his walet', presumably along with the pardons. Also 'him thoughte' it was the latest fashion, that is to say 'it seemed to him' – though, by implication, presumably to no one else. All in all, the Pardoner comes across as a vain, loud, lustful, effeminate, cunning, dishonest glutton.

But – and this is a big 'but' which turns our thoughts in an entirely different direction – as an exponent of his craft the Pardoner is second to none. In his topsy-turvy world, where the ability to cheat the poor is a measure of success, there is no one throughout the land who can match him. With a frankness which foreshadows the Pardoner's own Chaucer describes some of his false 'relics' – a pillowcase which he says is Our Lady's veil, a fragment of St Peter's sail, an ancient-looking crucifix, and pigs' bones in a jar. These are just a sample, just a few of the means by which he wins his huge profits, as he describes more fully in his own *Prologue* (see section 4.4). If he can find a gullible country parson and hijack his congregation, he can make more money in a day than the parson earns in two whole months, and in this way, by the narrow values of this world at least, he makes fools of them all.

With a protestation of earnestness, the final judgement is delivered:

> But trewely to tellen atte laste.
> He was in chirche a noble ecclesiaste. (707–8)

'How can this be?' we ask. Hasn't he been shown to lack every moral and even physical attribute we might reasonably expect in a man of the church? Is this a bland expression of misdirected approval? Or is Chaucer just saying the opposite of what he means? The answer is that when Chaucer makes such statements, as he does, for instance, of the Monk and the Friar, there is usually at least a grain of truth The Monk, for all his shortcomings, literally is 'a fair prelaat' ('a fine churchman'), not in the sense that he serves the church well but that he is a fine figure of a man, a sportsman who keeps himself in good physical shape. In the same ironic way the Pardoner's excellence lies narrowly in his church performances. He too cuts a fine figure and reads well from the scriptures and stories of saints. But best of all is his singing of the offertory anthem which precedes his sermon, for he knows his skills and is confident that he will make a lot of money for himself. So Chaucer leaves us, for the time being, with a mental picture of this unctuous cheat, singing 'the murierly and loude' in cynical anticipation of rich takings. How good of him to arrange for the Pardoner to have his comeuppance elsewhere in *The Canterbury Tales*!

4.2 THE PARDONER AND THE WIFE OF BATH

Another appearance of the Pardoner in *The Canterbury Tales* occurs when he interrupts the Wife of Bath during the prologue to her tale

(III, lines 163–87). The Wife has just cited the Epistle of St. Paul which urges men to love their wives, when up starts the Pardoner and congratulates her for being a 'noble prechour'. He says that he himself was about to take a wife but wonders whether he can now bring himself to do so in view of all that the Wife has said about the sorrows of matrimony. The Wife tells him that more is to come, for she is going to describe at greater length the tribulation that there is in marriage – something, she predicts, which will 'savoure wors than ale'. 'Madame, tell on', says the Pardoner deferentially, 'and teach us young men some of your practical wisdom'.

This seems a strangely inconsequential incident, though it does give the Wife the opportunity to anticipate what she is going to say, as well as contributing further to the picture of the Pardoner. It is worth noting that he is described in terms which are consistent with his characterisation elsewhere; his implied fondness for women, his description of himself as a young man, and even the Wife's hint that he has a liking for ale, are all perfectly in keeping with information given in other parts of *The Canterbury Tales*. Probably Chaucer introduced this little incident as another contribution to the dramatic context of the tales.

4.3 THE PARDONER'S HEADLINK

As mentioned before, some of the linking pieces between various of the tales seem to have been written by someone other than Chaucer. However, the Pardoner's headlink – which includes the Host's request for him to tell a tale, the outcry of the gentlefolk when they fear that the tale will be low and crude, and the Pardoner's request for time to take some refreshment while he is thinking of a worth-while story – is wholly Chaucerian and can be taken as an integral part of the introduction.

The Physician has just told the tragic story of the virtuous Virginia, who chose to die rather than endure the attentions of someone she did not love. Harry Bailly, the Host, extravagantly claims to have been so affected that he has almost had a heart attack; he will lose his heart for pity unless he has a healing medicine (an appropriate backward reference to the Physician) or a drink of 'moyste and corny ale'. Without hesitation he turns to the Pardoner with a request for 'myrthe or japes'. This request tells us something about the Pardoner, or at least about Harry Bailly's opinion of him, for it might on the face of it seem surprising that an officer of the church should be called upon to tell a saucy story. The Pardoner, however, does not object, even when the Host uses the condescending and rather disparaging term of address 'beel amy'. But the other pilgrims also have a pretty clear idea of the depravity of which the Pardoner is capable, for straightway the *gentils* protest that they do not want to hear anything indecent, but rather some edifying 'moral thyng'. The Pardoner complies, but asks for time to think up 'som honest thyng' to tell.

This, of course, is a pretence, for the Pardoner's tale turns out to be a well-rehearsed sermon from his professional repertoire. Certainly he would have delivered it hundreds of times before; he says at the end of his prologue that this is a tale 'which I am wont to preche'. Why, then, does he ask for time to think? Possibly Chaucer wishes to stress the Pardoner's liking for alcohol and to hint that he is garrulous and overconfident because of the ale has has been drinking; certainly there is a definite concentration of references to ale-drinking in the headlink, with another at the end of the Pardoner's prologue; and we have already noticed that his glaring eyes may betoken a drunkard. But whether or not this is so, this preparatory anecdote certainly helps build the dramatic context for the tale. It is not simply *any* tale, detached from people and events; it is the Pardoner's own, set in a context which is carefully contrived.

4.4 *THE PARDONER'S PROLOGUE*

The Pardoner's Prologue is wholly a self-revelation – not a confession, for the Pardoner is incapable of feeling a flicker of shame or remorse, but an acknowledgement of wicked intentions, rather like those of *Othello*'s Iago or even a Musical Hall villain, but without the pretence of confidentiality which gives at least a hint that the speaker knows he is doing wrong. The Pardoner is a sinner and he is proud of it. He condemns himself, and our sense of outrage is therefore all the greater.

He is totally aware of what he is about – in the material sense, at least – and begins by describing his preaching technique with an air of excited boastfulness (lines 329–46). First, he says, he assumes an impressive style of speech; next he announces his theme in Latin: *Radix malorum est cupiditas*, 'the desire for money is the root of all evil'; then he displays his letters and seals of authorisation; then he throws in a few more impressive-sounding Latin terms. (Section 7.1 contains a detailed analysis of this passage.) And then, with the manner of a magician performing to a party of eager children, he brings out his relics. The effect is predictable: his audience is hooked.

It may help to know what holy relics were, and how they came about, and how they were used and abused in medieval times. A relic is an object, commonly part of the body or clothing, venerated as a memorial to some departed saint or person of holy life. They were owned by institutions and by individuals; an example is Chaucer's patron, Edward III, who possessed several boxes of them – the ecclesiastical vestments of St Edward the Confessor, an armbone of St Amphibalis, some of the blood of St George, a tooth of St Adrian, part of the post to which Christ was tied when he was whipped, and so on. Belief in the power of Christian relics developed soon after the death of Christ and was often linked with legendary tales, such as that of St Helena's supposed discovery of the cross on which Jesus died. Miraculous cures and events were said to have happened to those who had touched this cross, and it seems that all the faithful wished to see it or touch it or possess a piece of it for themselves. In Chaucer's day if all the pieces of wood which were claimed to be fragments of the true cross had been gathered together they would have filled many waggons and have been sufficient for hundreds of crosses. But people were credulous, and even respectable churchmen were disinclined to question too deeply, since it was of great benefit for a church to possess famous relics – the more the better – as they would attract pilgrims who would make generous offerings. Obviously the system was open to abuse, and the Pardoner, who patently has no belief in the efficacy of his 'rags and bones', was just one of the many who took advantage.

Our Pardoner's relics have already been briefly referred to in the *General Prologue*. Now we are told how they are put to use (lines 347–90). The act starts with a display of his crystal reliquaries, boxes or jars designed to house the relics and, by their ornateness, to emphasise the holiness of what they contain. The Pardoner cheerfully admits that they are 'crammed full of rags and bones'; but to the people they are holy relics – 'or so they all think', he adds. Then he picks out an old bone set in brass. This, he says, is the shoulder-bone of the sheep of a 'holy Jew', a preposterous claim which he leaves shrouded in vagueness. Any water in which this bone has been washed has marvellous healing qualities, and if a peasant-farmer drinks some of it once a week at the crack of dawn his prosperity is assured (here he plays on the very *cupiditas* against which he pretends to be preaching). This bone has yet another remarkable quality, for if the water is used in a man's soup he shall lose all sense of jealousy and never again mistrust his wife, even if he is certain of her misbehaviour with other men. By this means the Pardoner is able to hold out the prospect of a life of uninterrupted adultery to all the country wives who take up his offer. Also amongst his junk he has a mitten, and to anyone who places his hand inside he promises a successful harvest of grain – provided that he first makes a money offering to the Pardoner, of course.

As if all this were not enough, he has a special *gaude*, 'trick', which virtually guarantees him a rich haul. He warns that if anyone in his congregation is guilty of some 'synne horrible' and is ashamed to confess and atone for it, or if any woman has made a cuckold of her husband, such miscreants will be denied the chance to come up and make a donation, for only those free from such deadly sin may come forward and take advantage of his offer. This, of course, is thinly-veiled blackmail, for a man or woman who did not go up would, under the circumstances, run the risk of being branded a secret sinner; so even those who might be sceptical of the Pardoner would feel disinclined to remain in their seats. By means of this trick, he says, he has earned himself a fortune:

> By this gaude have I wonne, yeer by yeer,
> An hundred mark sith I was pardoner. (389–90)

The last part of his prologue (lines 391–462), for all its apparent coherence, is found on investigation to be strangely rambling. Three main themes are intertwined, and each is left and returned to as new lines of thought are followed up. Firstly there is the continued description of the Pardoner's technique. His excitement seems to rise as he pictures himself stretching out his neck and turning his head this way and that like a dove sitting on a barn – an image as physically apt as it is imaginatively inapt, since the dove stood for truth and love. In a paroxysm of childish vanity he declares:

> Myne handes and my tonge goon so yerne
> That it is joye to se my bisynesse. (398–9)

This proccupation with his preaching method is then abandoned until line 435, where he describes how he makes liberal use of old stories that people can easily understand and repeat.

The second theme the Pardoner introduces is that good sermons can be delivered for bad reasons. Lots of people do it, he claims, for reasons of flattery, self-agrandisement, or out of hatred. He himself takes advantage of the opportunity the pulpit affords him to slander the detractors of his fellow pardoners and himself. Without mentioning any names he can make it quite clear to whom he is referring, and

> Thus spitte I out my venym under hewe
> Of hoolynesse, to semen hooly and trewe. (421–2)

This theme is also left for a while and then taken up again when at line 429 he says that although he himself is a cynical hypocrite he may still be the agent of salvation for others:

> But though myself be gilty in that synne,
> Yet kan I maken oother folk to twynne
> From avarice, and soore to repente. (429–31)

Thirdly, the Pardoner returns again and again to his opening theme, *Radix malorum est Cupiditas,* and to the great joke (as he sees it) that he himself is supremely guilty of the sin which he most condemns. *Cupiditas* is simply the Latin word for 'avarice' or 'coveityse', both of which keep cropping up. 'I always preach about avarice', he says, to make them generous in giving – 'and namely ['especially'] unto me' (402) – because I only care about profits, and not at all about the good of souls.' Then again:

> I preche of no thyng but for coveityse. (424)

And again, in almost the same words:

> I preche nothyng but for coveitise, (433)

after which either he or Chaucer seems to sense that the point is in danger of being overpressed, for he adds:

> Of this mateere it oughte ynogh suffise. (434)

But this is not the end of it. *Cupiditas* is so all-consuming in the Pardoner that he now rises to a crescendo of indignation at the mere idea that he should earn his living by respectable means. 'I *will* have money, wool, cheese and wheat,' he asserts (using emphatic *wol*, meaning 'want to, intend to'),'even if it is given by the poorest serving-boy or widow in a village'; even if her children should have to starve, he himself intends, with shocking excess, to drink 'licour of the vyne' (452) and to have a 'joly wench' in every town. (This last assertion may seem odd in view of the Pardoner's unusual sexual make-up, but it would have signalled the sin of lechery clearly enough).

And then, in the middle of a couplet at line 454, he breaks off and returns to the subject of the pilgrims and his tale. The effect of this seems to suggest that he had fallen into a sort of ecstasy from which he only now pulls himself. 'Though I myself', he says, 'am a very *vicious* ['wicked'] man, none the less I know how to tell a moral tale [that theme again], and it is one which I am accustomed to preach for profit [that theme again, too], and now I will begin'.

No one could claim, then, that *The Pardoner's Prologue* is not emphatic in its reiteration of a restricted range of themes, and any reader of the tale or interpreter of the Pardoner's character would be foolish to ignore such strong accentuation. It is clearly not Chaucer's intention to develop the Pardoner merely by suggestion. So black a villain is obviously not very realistic, and the figure to emerge from *The Pardoner's Prologue* is much more of a stereotypical villain than a psychologically believable character. Is it not therefore wrong to interpret his other antics (such as his later attempt to sell his relics to the pilgrims) in psychological terms? And to what extent does the boldly-drawn figure of the Pardoner overshadow and dominate the tale which he now goes on to tell?

4.5 *THE PARDONER'S TALE*

Summary
The tale is about a group of young people in Flanders who lead a life of shocking debauchery – gambling, fornicating, swearing, revelling, and eating and drinking to excess. Almost as soon as he has introduced them the Pardoner launches into a lengthy expression of moral indignation, first concerning drunkenness and gluttony, then gambling and swearing, in which he has recourse to a succession of *exempla* (allusions to well-known exemplary tales) and to Biblical and traditional authorities by whom these evils are condemned. As the tale continues we find three of these *riotoures* drinking in a tavern early one morning when they hear a funeral cortège passing by. They learn that an old friend has died at the hands of a 'privee theef' named Death, who has been responsible for killing many others in that region. In a drunken rage the three swear an oath of brother-hood and set off together to bring Death to a quick end.

Before they get very far they meet an old man, whom they abuse and accuse of being in league with Death. The old man denies it, but tells them where they can find Death, if they are so set in that purpose. Off they rush to the place, but instead of their adversary they find a heap of gold florins under an oak tree. All thoughts of their quest now vanish as they rapturously contemplate the lives of luxurious debauchery they will now be able to lead.

The treasure must be taken home under the cover of night, so in the meantime the youngest is dispatched to town to fetch bread and wine. In his absence the remaining two make a plan to kill him upon his return and to keep his share for themselves; but the man on the errand is also overcome by greed, and puts poison in the wine he has brought for them. He is attacked and killed, and the others, after celebrating with a drink, meet their deaths by poisoning. After a final expression of moral outrage the Pardoner exhorts his listeners to come forward to buy pardons. Seemingly this is part of his regular performance, for he goes on to offer his services specifically to his fellow pilgrims (see section 4.6).

The setting (lines 463–82)
From the outset the story has the unmistakeable features of a moral tale, for the catalogue of outrages with which it begins obviously points forward to a grisly reversal. The young revellers are not individually drawn. Nowhere in the tale are they given names, and we do not even know how many of them there are until much later, when they are casually referred to as 'thise riotoures thre' (661). They are simply designated 'one of them' (666), 'the third' (836), 'the proudest' (716), 'the worst' (776), 'the youngest' (804), and so on; but this is specific enough, for they are meant to be exemplary, not realistic. We are told straightforwardly enough what they get up to – having a good time, gambling, visiting brothels and taverns, cursing, swearing, keeping the very worst company, and generally leading lives of unrelieved debauchery – and we are encouraged to see them as representatives of the sum total of all these vices, namely 'folye' (464) and 'superfluytee', 'excess' (471). Chaucer's public, which was more trained in such matters, would instantly have thought of the deadly sins which these excesses indicate (see section 5.2). The tale, then, is about sin; and everyone knows (and certainly knew then) that the wages of sin is death.

The Pardoner's digression on gluttony (lines 483–588)
But the Pardoner is not the sort merely to hint at a moral point when he can thunder it home with a rhetorical flourish, and he now embarks upon a long digression in condemnation of the most blatant of the evils which these Flemish revellers exemplify. He begins with the deadly sin of gluttony, and includes a few sideswipes at drunkenness, which is a branch of it. In effect he preaches a sort of sub-sermon, on the text (based on St Paul's Epistle to the Ephesians) that 'luxurie is

in wyn and dronkenesse' (484), where 'luxurie' means 'excess', with overtones particularly of lechery. The technique is typical of medieval sermons (see section 6.3). Two *exempla* provide instances of famous people who illustrate the point: Lot, who committed incest, and Herod, who gave the order for John the Baptist to be beheaded, both acting under the influence of drink. Then an *authority* on the subject is cited, the Roman philosopher Seneca, who wrote about the similarity between drunkenness and madness. Then an *apostrophe*:

> O glotonye, ful of cursednesse!
> O cause first of oure confusion! (498–9),

which leads to another *exemplum*, that of Adam and Eve who ate the apple of the forbidden tree, a gluttonous act. To maintain the rhetorical tone at its feverish level, more apostrophes follow, then a patchwork of quotation and paraphrase skilfully pieced together from famous authors: 'Allas! the shorte throte' (517), from St Jerome or Pope Innocent III; 'Mete unto wombe, and wombe eek unto mete' (522), from St Paul's first *Epistle to the Corinthians*; 'Of his throte he maketh his pryvee' (527), also from St Jerome; and 'wombe is hir god' (533), from St Paul's *Epistle to the Philippians*. The Pardoner claims to have been moved to tears by the thought of all this (243), and certainly the high-sounding rhetoric seems to suggest emotional involvement, though we know this is pretended rather than real.

Mundane words like *cod* ('bag') and *dong* ('dung') contrast effectively with the lofty style as the Pardoner now turns his attention to the excesses of *haute cuisine*:

> O wombe! O bely! O stynkyng cod!
> Fulfilled of dong and of corrupcion!
> At either ende of thee foul is the soun. (534–6)

In dealing with the labour and expense which are caused by gluttony, the Pardoner makes rather less use of established authors, though the scholarly joke that cooks merely turn 'substunce into accident' (539) (that is to say, they change the plain ingredients into something highly artificial), was probably borrowed from the writings of Pope Innocent III. The picture of cooks, stamping and straining and grinding to serve the appetites of their masters, who in medieval times demanded dishes of extraordinary delicacy, recalls the portrait of the Cook in the *General Prologue*, whilst Chaucer's Franklin, in whose house it 'snowed' food and drink, suggests to us the sort of glutton whose appetite would be served by all this.

The digression on drunkenness (lines 549–88)
Shifting ground slightly, the Pardoner now turns the focus more specifically on the related sin of drunkenness. This passage is analysed in detail in section 7.2.

The digression on gambling (lines 589–628)
A more substantial change of subject comes when the theme of gambling is taken up. The mechanical way in which the change is accomplished ('Now that I have finished speaking about gluttony I am going on to speak against your having anything to do with gambling') recalls actual preaching practice, for sermons were usually very rigidly structured, and changes in subject were strongly emphasised for reasons of clarity; but there is also a suggestion that the Pardoner is mechanically working his way through the stages of his 'performance', and that he is more cynically detached than his manner would suggest.

Gambling was condemned, as the Pardoner says, for the many sins with which it was associated: lying, deception, perjury, blasphemy, manslaughter and waste. Among princes gambling was especially despised, as the works of instruction for princes, the so-called 'Mirrors for Princes', taught. Again the point is made through the use of *exempla*: firstly the story of Chilon, the Lacedemonian ambassador (here he is mistakenly called *Stilboun*), who refused to make an alliance with the Corinthians because they were a nation of gamblers; and secondly the story of the gift by the king of the Parthians to King Demetrius of a pair of golden dice in scorn of his gambling habits. The Pardoner gives extra weight to his preaching by referring to the authority of a 'wise philosophre' (620) for his first story and to some unspecified source, 'the book' (622), for his second.

The digression on swearing (lines 629–59)
In the same mechanical manner as before the Pardoner now shifts his ground to tackle the sin of swearing 'of othes false and grete' (629). He calls again on the authority of 'olde bookes' (630), though all his examples are taken from the Bible. Here he is able to mention the most potent prohibition of all, the condemnation of swearing spoken by Jesus himself, as described in the Gospel of Matthew. The rest is Old Testament support – from the words of the prophet Jeremiah (634–7), from the second of the Ten Commandments, which forbids taking the name of God in vain (639–47), and from the Book of Ecclesiasticus (649–50). Then comes a little act, in which he assumes the role of one who swears 'by God's precious heart', 'by God's nails', 'by the blood of Christ at Hailes' (a reference to a supposed

holy relic at the abbey of that name in Gloucestershire) and 'by God's arms'. These oaths upon the body of God and Christ (for 'nails', though originally the Crucifixion nails, came to be thought of as Christ's fingernails), are the sort which, as it were, 'tear to pieces' the holy body – something the Pardoner has already condemned in the *riotoures* at the start of the tale (474). So after this substantial digression we have been cleverly led back to the subject of the tale, with which the Pardoner now continues.

The quest for Death (lines 661–710)

The focus is narrowed to three of the *riotoures*, but in them the polarisation of good and evil is just as clear as before. The three have made an early start to the day's drinking, for long before the bell of 'prime' they are already in the tavern. 'Prime' was the six o'clock church service, and the mention of this reminds us of an ordered religious life very different from that which these men are leading in the 'develes temple' (470). A funeral procession passes, and churlishly one of the men orders his serving-boy to find out who has died. The boy already knows that the dead man is an old friend of theirs and that the culprit is a sneak-thief named Death, who has taken many other lives throughout the region. The boy has a healthy respect for him, as would all medieval people who had lived through the sort of plague which is referred to in line 679, for which it is said that Death is responsible. From sermons, books and pictures all medieval people would have learned about Death's sudden coming (673), his spear (677), the uselessness of contending with him (682), and his equal treatment of all types of people. The sentiments of the boy and the tavern-keeper express traditional wisdom about him:

> Beth redy for to meete hym everemoore;
> Thus taughte me my dame; I sey namoore. (684–5)

It is a sign of the moral blindness of the *riotoures* that they have no understanding of this familiar personification or of the dreadful inevitably of his coming. So, with a flurry of blasphemous curses, they now swear an oath of brotherhood, ironically pledging to live and die for each other, and set off to find Death and to kill him that very day. (For more on the personification of Death see section 5.4.)

The old man (lines 711–59)

They have hardly begun their quest when they come across an old man, a strange and pathetic figure, yet at the same time uncanny and disturbing. Scholars have found parallels to him in folktales throughout the world, and have tended to be preoccupied with his origins and with what he represents. However, it is much more useful to think about what his *function* is in the tale. Obviously he helps keep the theme of death very much in mind, for he even looks like a corpse, being wrapped up with only his face exposed, like a dead body in a shroud. He is therefore a sort of *memento mori*, a reminder of death which medieval people used to help concentrate their thoughts upon virtue (see section 5.4). He plays a similar role to the character called Age in the Morality Plays, whose function is to warn of the nearness of Death. Another of his functions is to teach the *riotoures* where to find Death, not because he is in league with him, as one of them claims, but because he has a mature understanding of living and dying which the younger men lack, and knows the traditional teachings about death. This lies behind his resignation to the will of God (726), behind his desire to return to his 'mother earth' (731, 734), from which mortal man was born (as Adam is said to have been fashioned from clay) and to which he must return, and behind his teachings about the respect which young people should pay to the old, which he backs up with quoted Biblical authority (739–47). Yet another of his functions is to act as a contrast to the others and through his simple wisdom to accentuate their arrogant folly. So, for example, his extreme age is stressed in contrast to their youth, his courtesy and mildness in contrast to their rudeness and aggression, and his long search for a final resting-place in contrast to their rash quest to find death of a different kind. It is here, in these rich layers of parallels and contrasts, that some of the most delicious irony is to be found. (Part of this and of the next section are analysed further in 7.3 below.)

The treasure (lines 760–805)

The old man reluctantly points out where they can find Death and off they rush, only to discover, not the villain they have been seeking, but a heap of golden florins in mint condition. Perhaps the most richly ironic line of the whole tale comes here:

> No lenger thanne after Deeth they soughte, (772)

for at the moment when it seems that they have given up the quest they have, of course, found him. With the discovery of this treasure the theme of avarice, which has been absent for some time, is emphatically reintroduced.

After a brief period of euphoria, which is vividly yet economically described, the ringleader's thoughts turn to the furtive measures necessary to retain this new-found wealth. 'The treasure is ours to enjoy', he says, with dubious logic, 'because Fortune has given it to us'; 'if it might be carried home to my house all would be well' ('or elles unto youres,' he adds (785), as an afterthought to cover his selfish greed); 'but if we were to be seen carrying it, people would accuse us of theft and have us hanged', ('for oure owene tresor,' he says, with ridiculous moral indignation); 'therefore it must be carried home at night' (already his earlier bluster has changed to the furtiveness which characterises the miser); 'so let one of us, chosen by lot, go for food and drink, and the others stay here on guard.' The plan is so swiftly enacted that we are not even told how this idea was received, merely that the youngest drew the short straw and was despatched for the food and drink.

Death shows his hand (lines 806–94)

As the focus narrows on the two remaining *riotoures*, we come to learn of their true feelings and of the shocking lengths to which they are prepared to go to satisfy their greedy desires. The ringleader approaches the other who has been left on guard with a reminder that they are sworn brothers; this is again ironic, since so also is the third, whose life he now plans to take with little thought of the brotherhood they have pledged. In contrast to the former rapid unfolding of the plan, this part moves slowly, perhaps reflecting the hesitancy of the two men to reveal their true feelings one to another. But with their greed laid bare, they agree to murder the other upon his return and for this damnable crime, which would cost their souls without doubt an eternity in hell, they can think of nothing better than the pathetic indulgence of a few worldly pleasures:

> Thanne may we bothe oure lustes all fulfille,
> And pleye at dees right at oure owene wille. (833–4)

But the one who has been sent to town, the youngest, is no better. Greed has overtaken him, too:

> Ful ofte in herte he rolleth up and doun
> The beautee of thise floryns newe and brighte. (838–9)

And in this mental state he is susceptible to a wicked thought implanted by the devil. We see the plan to poison his fellows grow quickly from a mere thought to a firm resolve:

> For this was outrely his fulle entente,
> To sleen hem bothe, and nevere to repente. (849–50)

Then, quite surprisingly, for the narrative has been very fast-moving so far (apart from the Pardoner's rhetorical digressions), as many as seventeen lines are given over to the scene in which the man buys poison from an apothecary after telling elaborate lies about the vermin which have been troubling him, and to the apothecary's description of the efficacy and violence of his poison, while a further eleven lines are used to describe the preparation of the bottles. The effect of this slowing of the narrative is to emphasise, by contrast, the speedy outcome. The Pardoner does not even bother to describe the stabbing to death of the youngest by the other two; he merely offers it as a foregone conclusion:

> What nedeth it to sermone of it moore?
> For right as they hadde cast his deeth bifoore,
> Right so they han hym slayn, and that anon. (879–81)

And the poisoning of the others is presented in an equally cursory way: each simply takes a drink from a poisoned bottle,

> For which anon they storven bothe two. (888)

It is almost as an afterthought that the Pardoner hints at the ferocious effects of the poison. Avicenna, the famous Arab philosopher and writer on medicine, apparently never described in any of his books clearer symptoms of poisoning than the two corpses showed in this instance. In this way the Pardoner not only airs his knowledge once again by yet another learned allusion, but also relieves himself of the need to go into detail; to suggest the gory picture in this way is so much more effective than to describe it.

A final rhetorical flourish (lines 895–903)
And so the tale is ended, though not before the Pardoner makes a final rhetorical flourish, apostrophising the 'cursed synne of alle cursednesse' (i.e. 'the most grievous sin of all', presumably avarice), the murderous traitors, gluttony, excess, gambling, blasphemy, and (for good measure) wickedness in general. It is characteristic that the Pardoner should contrive to end on a high note.

4.6   THE EPILOGUE

But this is not quite the end, for there now follows a kind of appendix, an Epilogue, which has caused more discussion than any other part of the *Prologue* or *Tale*.

Once again the Pardoner reverts to the subject of his pardons, and now he makes more extravagant claims for them than any he has made hitherto. By means of them, he claims, he can 'warice' ('redeem', 906) all those who are prepared to pay; the names of those who offer money or goods will be entered in his prayer-roll (911), which he seems to think of as a list of saved souls, like that from which the archangel Michael will read at the Day of Doom; and, assuming quite improperly the status of a priest, he offers to 'assoille' ('absolve from sin', 913). 'And lo, sires, thus I preche,' he says (915), revealing that he has only now come to the end of the set sermon which he is accustomed to preach.

Since the stage has been reached at which the Pardoner is again talking directly to his fellow pilgrims, it is extraordinary that he should now attempt to get money from them for the use of pardons and relics that he has only just shown to be worthless. He introduces the subject as an afterthought: it occurs to him that he has pardons in his bag which they may come forward and receive right now, or else take 'newe and fressh at every miles ende' (928), as long as they are prepared to pay. Furthermore, it is an honour, he says, for them to have such a Pardoner at hand, as well as a kind of life insurance, for if they should meet with a fatal accident along the way he will be on hand to offer absolution.

This inconsequential offer from a man who has already shown himself to be a fraud has puzzled generations of readers, and no one has yet offered a totally satisfactory explanation. Some, remembering his liking for ale, have claimed that he is too drunk to know what he is doing; others that he is intoxicated by his own performance; or that he sees how the pilgrims are affected by his tale and seizes the chance to capitalise on it; or that he arrogantly assumes that his powers of persuasion are so great that he can wring money even from those to whom he has just revealed his trickery; or that he is joking, and not seriously offering his services at all; or, conversely, that he is being momentarily sincere. This last interpretation relies very much upon what the Pardoner says immediately before his offer to the pilgrims:

> And Jhesu Crist, that is oure soules leche,
> So graunte yow his pardoun to receyve,
> For that is best; I wol yow nat deceyve. (916–18)

This point takes us back to lines 429–31 of *The Pardoner's Prologue*, where he says that though he himself is guilty of avarice, nevertheless he has the power to make others turn away from that sin. So possibly the Pardoner is offering what he believes to be genuinely efficacious services to the pilgrims irrespective of his own base motives. The problem with this, as with all the explanations summarised above, is that it relies too heavily upon a 'psychological' interpretation of a character who is not otherwise depicted realistically or given any psychological depth. But this explanation, unlike most of the others, does at least make use of evidence from within the text.

One further explanation (and there are still more) is that Chaucer was prepared to dispense with considerations of realism in the interests of building up the dramatic context. We have already noticed that the Pardoner is an 'interactive' character – he sings with the Summoner and interrupts the Wife of Bath, for instance. In the Pardoner's *Headlink* there is a conversation between the Host, the Pardoner, and the gentlefolk, while in the *Epilogue* the Host, the Pardoner and the Knight are involved; elsewhere in *The Canterbury Tales* it is unusual for conversations involving more than two characters to occur. So Chaucer seems to have used the Pardoner as a key figure in the dramatic framework of the tales. What is more natural, then, than that he should have devised the little incident of his Epilogue, irrespective of the Pardoner's exact motives, as an emphatic end to his tale?

Considerations of psychological realism would surely have prevented the Pardoner from turning first to the Host for an offering, and from characterising him as 'moost envoluped in synne' (942), for Harry Bailly is a bluff and hearty character who stands no nonsense and does not mince his words. But this is what the Pardoner does, and not surprisingly he is met with a firm rebuff. Swearing by a true relic, the cross which St Helena found, the Host declares that he would rather lay his hand on the Pardoner's testicles enshrined in hog's dung than on any of his phoney 'relics' in their crystal reliquaries. Understandably the Pardoner is speechless with rage, perhaps all the more so because the Host's remarks hint at his lack of virility. But surprisingly the remarks seem to have been not unkindly meant, for Harry Bailly says that he 'no lenger' wishes to 'pleye' ('have fun') with the Pardoner or with any other angry man, at which the Knight intervenes and gets them to kiss and make up. So all ends pleasantly enough.

5 MAJOR THEMES

5.1 A MORAL TALE

The Pardoner promises to tell a moral tale and in this he does not
disappoint. There can be no doubt about its serious moral purpose,
which shines through despite the Pardoner's cynicism, and is even
enhanced by it.

In medieval works the moral lesson is frequently much more
explicit than in modern writings. Some medieval works even include
a section specified as being 'the moral' or 'the signification'. One such
is the thirteenth-century *Bestiary*, a list of real and imaginary animals
with their supposed characteristics and the lessons to be learned from
them. The fox, for instance, is described as a cunning creature which
traps all manner of birds by its wily tricks, one of which involves
pretending to be dead so that it can suddenly leap up and seize the
carrion birds which have come to peck at its flesh; there are two
'significations': the first equates the fox with the devil, who ensnares
men and women through his deceptions, and the second likens both
the fox and the devil to those men and women who speak pleasantly
whilst thinking evil. Another thirteenth-century poem, sometimes
known as *Contempt of the World*, sketches a picture of beautiful
ladies in days gone by, and proud, rich men with their retinues, and
asks: 'What has become of them now?'; more than half the poem is
given over to the moral lesson that it is better to suffer hardships
briefly here on earth than to seek only pleasure and so win everlasting
suffering in hell. In Chaucer's own day his friend John Gower
(addressed once as 'Moral Gower' by Chaucer) wrote tales to
illustrate a range of moral teachings, like the story of *Jason and
Medea*, a tale of faithless love, which ends with the typical formula:

> Thus might thou see what sorrow it doth
> To swear an oath which is not sooth [*true*].

In those days drama also was used to convey explicit moral teachings: in some of the Mystery Plays there is a special 'expositor', whose role is to come forward from time to time and point out to the audience the significance of a particular event; and the Morality Plays (as the name implies), were even more overtly committed to a didactic purpose, such as the play *Everyman*, which begins and ends with explanatory moral speeches for which two characters, who have no other function in the play, are specially created. In all, then, medieval people loved a good tale, and if it had a strongly pointed moral then so much the better.

Sermons, of course, were among the most obviously moral of all medieval compositions, and in the case of the Pardoner's sermon the explicit moral is enshrined in the theme with which he begins:

> *Radix malorum est Cupiditas.* (334)

As was the case with most sermon texts, this is taken from the Bible, from St Paul's *First Letter to Timothy*, 6:10, and, having been drawn into proverbial use, it has the added authority of traditional wisdom. So in a narrow sense *The Pardoner's Tale* is a story, just as the Pardoner claims, designed to encourage

> folk to twynne
> From avarice, and soore to repente. (430–1)

But the prologue and tale mean more than this, for, unlike an ordinary sermon, this one has a dramatic context which gives it an additional moral dimension. In a limited sense the Pardoner himself recognises this, for he acknowledges that his own behaviour exemplifies the main sin against which he preaches:

> Thus kan I preche agayn that same vice
> Which that I use, and that is avarice. (427–8)

He sees his ability to cheat and win money as a mark of success. But obviously the other pilgrims do not see things this way; nor did Chaucer, and neither should we. If the Pardoner were not so steeped in vice he would be able to recognise where all this must inevitably lead him. He is a living text, a walking *exemplum*, a frightening example of a way of life which leads inexorably to the indescribable torments of hell. His prologue and tale therefore, form an insepar-able unit; without the one the value and impact of the other would be immeasurably decreased.

5.2 THE DEADLY SINS

Despite its text, which is the one the Pardoner always uses, *The Pardoner's Tale* does not merely deal with the sin of covetousness, but takes in gluttony, drunkenness, gambling, and swearing, as well as others which are not singled out for special attention. The most concentrated attention on specific abuses comes in the Pardoner's digression on the tavern vices immediately before the introduction of the three *riotoures*. It is normal to use the word digression to refer to this, but the term should not be understood to imply any departure from the subject in hand. Long 'asides' such as this were much more common in medieval storytelling than in narratives of today; but we should not allow the relative strangeness of this to distract our attention from its complete and essential connection with the matter in hand. As Ian Bishop has written in his essay on 'The Narrative Art of *The Pardoner's Tale*':

> The digression is, of course, entirely relevant to the *sentence* of the *exemplum* which it interrupts. Although Avarice is the radical sin that is illustrated in the tale, the three sins that are denounced in the digression – drunkenness, swearing and gambling – all contribute to the bringing about of the tale's catastrophe. If the rioters had not been drunk, they would not have set out upon their quest to 'sleen this false traytour Deeth' in the first place. If they had not been so profligate with their oaths, they might have taken more seriously their covenant of brotherhood and might have paid more attention to the solemn, admonitory imprecations of the old man. 'Hasar-drye' is obviously related to Avarice, but it is perhaps worth remarking that the habitual desire of each of the revellers to play for the highest possible stakes causes him to plot against one or both of his 'brothers' and so is directly responsible for inducing the internecine catastrophe.

Medieval views on these matters, and on right and wrong in general, were much more predetermined than our own. People's ideas were influenced by a widely known scheme for the classification of sin by kind (the family relationships of sin) and by degree (whether 'deadly sins' which, if unatoned for, would lead to damnation and death of the soul, or the lesser 'venial sins' which might entail a longer period than normal in Purgatory, the ante-room of heaven). The organisation of sins, and their corresponding virtues, was partly a natural consequence of the medieval world view, which saw everything as having its place, and also partly the result of the church's encouragement that people should think in this way. Every medieval Christian was obliged to confess his sins at least once a year, and to expedite the process for both penitent and priest, numerous handbooks were issued which encouraged people to think of sin in a systematic and logical way. Individual treatment of the details varied, but the main ideas were not in dispute. Seven 'deadly' sins were distinguished: Pride, Envy, Wrath, Sloth, Lechery, Gluttony and Covetousness. These were sometimes linked with the three great enemies of mankind, the World, the Flesh and the Devil. Covetousness was associated with the World; Sloth, Lechery and Gluttony with the Flesh; and Pride, Envy and Wrath with the Devil. Each sin also had numerous subdivisions, such as Pride, which in some schemes comprised Untruth, Despite, Presumption, Ambition, Vain Glory, Hypocrisy and Wicked Power; and even these might be subdivided, such as Presumption into Singularity, Prodigality, Foolish Undertaking, Boasting, Scorn and Rebellion. There were also 'remedies', or antidotes, to the sins: Humility to Pride, Love to Envy, Patience to Wrath, Strength (or Spiritual Joy) to Sloth, Chastity to Lechery, Abstinence to Gluttony, and Pity (or Liberality) to Covetousness, and these too had their subdivisions.

The classification of vices and virtues was no mere academic exercise, but one with which every individual would have been familiar, and which medieval preachers frequently expounded from the pulpit. Chaucer's *Parson's Tale*, in fact, does just this, for it is a long sermon in rambling prose on the theme of 'Penitence', most of which is taken up with a description of the sins and their remedies. Some of what is written there is directly relevant to *The Pardoner's Tale*. The three *riotoures*, it seems, most explicitly exemplify Wrath, which the Parson describes as follows:

O Ire ['Wrath'] comen thise stynkynge engendrures ['offspring']: First, hate, that is oold wratthe; discord, thurgh which a man forsaketh his olde freend that he hath loved ful longe; and thanne cometh werre, and every manere of wrong that man dooth to his neighbor, in body or in catel ['goods']. Of this cursed synne of Ire cometh eek manslaughtre. And understonde well that homycide . . . is manslaughtre . . . Yet comen ther of Ire manye mo synnes, as wel in word as in thoght and in dede, as he that arretteth upon ['grumbles against'] God, or blameth God of thyng of which he is hymself gilty, or despiseth God and alle his halwes ['saints'], as doon thise cursede hasardours in diverse contrees . . . After this, thanne cometh sweryng, that is expres agayn ['expressly against'] the comandement of God; and this bifalleth ofte of anger and of Ire . . . For Cristes sake, ne swereth nat so synfully in dismembrynge of Crist by soule, herte, bones, and body. For certes, it semeth that ye thynke that the cursede Jews ne dismembred nat ynough the precïouse persone of Crist, but ye dismembre hym moore.

The last point is one which the Pardoner makes in his own sermon (*Pardoner's Tale*, line 475). And there are other passages in *The Parson's Tale* which have the same familiar ring:

Glotonye is unmesurable appetit to ete or to drynke . . . This synne hath manye speces ['species']. The first is dronkenesse, that is the horrible sepulture ['grave, final resting place'] of mannes resoun . . . The seconde spece of glotony is that the spirit of a man wexeth ['grows'] al trouble ['disturbed'], for dronkenesse bireveth hym the discrecioun of his wit.

The point is this: not only is the Pardoner's a moral tale; it also illustrates the complex interrelationship and interdependence of one sin upon another; and it emphasises the damnation which must inevitably come to those who practise the deadly sins and set their faces against God. the Pardoner not only exemplifies avarice, for this is merely the most obvious of his wickednesses; but in terms of the church's teaching on the seven deadly sins he appears to encompass them all. Pride is all too clear in every facet of the Pardoner's performance; Envy can be seen in his 'false defaming' of his accusers (cf. *Pardoner's Prologue*, 415); Wrath is specifically mentioned as the Pardoner's reaction to Harry Bailly at the end of his tale (line 957); Sloth is shown by his scornful refusal to do any honest labour with his hands (*Pardoner's Prologue*, 444), and Gluttony and Lechery by his assertion that

I wol drynke licour of the vyne,
And have a joly wenche in every toun.

(*Pardoner's Prologue*, 452–3)

No doubt Chaucer did not mechanically develop the Pardoner simply to represent this range of sin, and some sins are obviously less important here than others. But it is as clear from the Pardoner himself as from the tale that one deadly sin is inevitably linked to another, for, as the Parson puts it in his tale, 'they all run in one leash', like a pack of hounds. The deadly sins are therefore as much the subject of *The Pardoner's Tale* as of *The Parson's Tale*. They help to define the moral and to extend its relevance to the teller of the tale and, by implication, to the real world beyond.

5.3 SPECIFIC ABUSES

The real world beyond was at that time probably no more corrupt than our own, though readers of *The Canterbury Tales* often take away the impression that it was, and that Chaucer often tried to expose specific abuses so that they might be reformed. The possibility that when he wrote *The Pardoner's Prologue* and *Tale* he had in mind a real scandal involving misappropriation of money collected on behalf of the hospital of Rouncivalle has been mentioned in section 4.1, but whether or not there was a specific model for this Pardoner is simply not known and must remain an open question. But the choice of his profession is a happy one, for if it was disreputable in Chaucer's day it went on to become totally discredited, for the sale of indulgences was the issue which split the church, and eventually the whole of the Christian world, when Martin Luther made his famous protest against them in 1517 and sparked off the Protestant Reformation. The friar Tetzel, whose arrival in Wittenburg to sell indulgences so fired Luther's indignation, was the real-life counterpart of Chaucer's Pardoner.

It has also been claimed that Chaucer harboured lollard sympathies, and that these can be detected in those writings in which he appears to be critical of the established church. The word 'lollard' originally meant 'idler', and was a disparaging term given by their enemies to the followers of the religious reformer John Wyclif, who objected to the complicated and sometimes corrupt institutions of the medieval church and urged a return to the plain teachings of the Bible. In some respects lollards were the medieval equivalents of the Puritans, with whom they shared a contempt for images and the pompous trappings of religious ceremony. Chaucer's one-time patron, John of Gaunt, was a supporter of Wyclif, and through him Wyclif and Chaucer may have become personally acquainted. Other of Chaucer's good friends were also keen supporters of lollardy, like Sir Lewis Clifford, who only recanted his views two years after Chaucer's death. But this does not make Chaucer a lollard himself, and the majority of his writings express the strictly orthodox ethical viewpoint which one would perhaps expect from such an 'establishment man' as a court poet and civil servant. The misgivings which he has are such as would have been shared by lollards and orthodox Catholics alike, for most thinking people at this time were conscious of abuses within the Church, which were almost inevitable in so vast an institution, which was a combination of major employer, provider of education, controller of the economy, supporter of government, regulator of the calendar, sanctifier of births, marriages and deaths, and source and arbiter of the moral laws and standards of the whole community. There was worldliness, misuse of wealth, exploitation of others, and so on; no one who has read *The General Prologue to The Canterbury Tales* could argue that Chaucer was oblivious of this, or that he was unaware of how often clerics fall below the ideal. But great churchmen like Saint Bernard and Saint Bonaventure had often been much more outspoken than Chaucer in their condemnation of abuse. Unlike these pillars of the church Chaucer preferred to question accepted truths with the humorous scepticism of one who was naturally critical and whose experience had been widened by travel abroad and by acquaintance with many interesting people of widely differing views. He provides no formally reasoned criticism, but responds either with deceptive playfulness or with disarming irony – but rarely with open antagonism – to the many absurdities and injustices he saw around him. For this reason *The Pardoner's Tale* impresses us as much with its serious moral as it delights us through the lively manner in which the moral is conveyed. Compare and contrast it with that pedestrianly moral sermon *The Parson's Tale* and it is easy to see why the one is still read and enjoyed while the other has been consigned to relative obscurity.

5.4 DEATH AND THE MACABRE

The macabre is perhaps more of a characteristic than a theme, but it is so pervasive in *The Pardoner's Tale* that it merits attention. Many writers on Chaucer have commented upon the uncanny weirdness of the tale, which one critic has called 'that magnificent retelling of an ancient plague legend, thick with gloomy and mysterious atmosphere'; but no one has quite been able to explain how this effect is achieved.

One possible explanation is to do with the tale's perspective. For much of the time – perhaps even all of the time – the *riotoures* are drunk. Either for this reason or because of their general depravity, they have lost their sense of reality. Their drink-crazed world is like that of a dream (the strange, unreal environment in which so many medieval poems are set), or of a nightmare in which normal values seem for the moment to be set aside. This is a world of corpses and lich-bells, of faceless people and shadowy personifications. The only character who is named is Death himself, an exception which only adds to the sense of unease. It is not that reality is totally absent: life and death, materialism and aggression are part of this world, for instance, and the very real horrors of the plague of Chaucer's time are brought home by the line

He hath a thousand slayn this pestilence (679)

and by the tavern keeper's description of the plague's obliteration of a complete village of people (686–8). But the problem for the revellers is that they have lost their ability to distinguish between the real and the unreal, the true and the false, the good and the bad.

Their problem of distinguishing is highlighted when they encounter the strange old man. Since generations of critics have been unable to agree just what he represents, it is hardly surprising that the *riotoures* cannot make him out. It seems to them unnatural that one so old should still be in the land of the living; but despite his long explanation they are quick to accuse him of being a spy sent to 'sleen us yonge folk'. In their world of half-truth, in which Death walks abroad, it is not surprising that they suspect this strange-looking figure to be a creature from the other world. Consequently they pay no attention to his good advice and show no respect for the years of experience which have turned him into the strange, shrunken figure he is. Instead they rush off to where the gold is awaiting them, immediately accept it as a gift of fortune, begin to plan their remaining years of luxury, and even plot murder as a means of increasing their own shares; yet they never stop to think what the treasure represents or how it got there. Presumably theirs is a world in which such unexpected events can happen in the normal course of things.

Another contributory factor to the uncanny atmosphere of the tale is the way in which detail is used. At one moment the narrative races along, such as at the beginning, where a generalised picture of the company of debauched young people in Flanders is quickly sketched; but at the next moment the story slows and a carefully chosen detail is mentioned. This technique is used elsewhere by Chaucer, for instance in the *General Prologue*: the Cook is a fairly anonymous character, but the sore on his leg is a detail which sticks in our memories, like the Knight's rusty armour, the wart on the nose of the

Miller with its tuft of red hairs, and the Wife of Bath's bright red stockings. Occasional factual details also stand out in *The Pardoner's Tale* – the funeral bell heard offstage as the cortège passes the tavern, the small detail that the dead man was taken as he sat 'upright' and drunk on a bench, and so on. A number of these details are associated with the old man. The *riotoures* meet him 'right as they wolde han troden over a stile'; he is 'al forwrapped' except for his face; he directs them 'up this croked wey' to the grove of trees, and points out one in particular:

Se ye that ook? Right there ye shal hym fynde. (765)

These details seems to take on an extra significance; they seem to be more than mere matters of chance, and to hint at powers far beyond the comprehension of the drunken *riotoures*, and tantalisingly just beyond the reader's as well.

Related to this is a disturbing sense that events in the tale have been predetermined, as if matters are proceeding according to the will of an unseen force. This is, of course, connected with the strong moral tone and with our knowledge that the tale is an *exemplum* of a sermon; we assume that right will assert itself and that sin will be punished. But in addition to this general sense of inevitability there is sometimes a coincidence of facts and events which suggests an extra element of retribution. One of the men gruffly tells his serving-boy to enquire the name of the dead man; but there is no need to enquire, for the boy already knows. The old man wearily anticipates their eagerness to find Death, and reluctantly directs them; from wise experience he could easily have warned them further, but that would have unbalanced the tale and detracted from his role as an agent of retribution. Even the apothecary's ready and full compliance with the youngest man's request for poison adds to the sense of inexorable necessity which drives the tale relentlessly to its conclusion.

However, the part of the tale with which the macabre element is most strongly associated is naturally the quest for Death itself, a theme which fits so satisfyingly that one would hardly guess that it is an addition to the basic story, perhaps introduced by Chaucer himself, for no trace of it is found in the analogues (see section 6.2).

In the fourteenth and fifteenth centuries death became an obsessive preoccupation, perhaps because the imminence of plague, which was sometimes known as 'the death', kept it to the forefront of people's minds. Death came to occupy a more prominent place in church doctrine, and became an important theme in art, literature and drama, which taught that the whole of life, in a sense, is a preparation for death. From the pulpit, through the counselling of confessors, and in the numerous devotional manuals on the *ars moriendi*, 'the art of dying', the faithful were taught to make themselves ready for death by regular contemplation of the 'last things' – heaven, hell, the grave, the corruption of the flesh, and the certainty of redemption through Christ. Images on tombes and gravestones often proclaimed the inevitability of death; some of the great men who could afford it arranged in advance for effigies of themselves resplendent in their finest robes to be set above a skeleton or mouldering corpse, as a reminder to those who would pass by the tomb in future years that the rich and powerful are eventually reduced by death to the same miserable condition as ordinary men.

Art and literature served the same ends, often utilising specific conventions connected with death, such as the personification of death, the idea that human life is a pilgrimage to the next world, and the motif of the Dance of Death, a macabre procession in which gleeful skeletons dance along to the grave with men and women of all ranks (but usually high temporal and spiritual lords) as their unwilling partners. But it is the drama in which the most chilling images are found, most famously in the Morality Play *Everyman*, in which Death appears to Everyman when he least expects it and 'arrests' him so that he can appear before God and give an account of his life. It is also in the drama that the closest parallel to the theme of death in *The Pardoner's Tale* occurs. In the morality play *The Pride of Life* (which survives only as a five-hundred-line fragment) a King of Life, who is a proud and strong temporal ruler, learns that a mysterious character called Death is oppressing the people and refusing to spare 'knight, caesar nor king'. The Queen and a Bishop advise the King to prepare his soul to meet Death, but the King scorns their advice and calls up his knights Strength and Health in preparation for a fight:

> Qhwat, prechistou of Dethis might
> and of his maistrye?
> He ne durst onis with me fight
> for his bothe eye!
>
> Streinth and Hele, qwhat sey ye,
> my kinde korin knightes?
> Schal Deth be lord over me
> And reve me of mightes?

[What, are you preaching about Death and his strength? He would not dare to fight once with me – not to save both his eyes!

Strength and Health, my own chosen knights, what do you say?
Shall Death be lord over me and deprive me of my powers?]

The last part of the play is missing, but the summary in the prologue
fills in the outline of the plot, describing how Death arrives and
overcomes the King, whose soul is only saved from hell by the
intercession of the Virgin Mary. The King apparently does not go off
in search of Death, so the quest theme is not present, but the general
similarity to *The Pardoner's Tale* is not difficult to see.

Chaucer, then, has done what is typical of him. He has utilised
familiar images of death in an original way, skilfully adapted them to
suit the needs of the tale, overlaid them with a multi-faceted irony
which invites us to contemplate the many forms and faces of death,
and related all this to a totally orthodox moral. In doing so he shows
that ability to treat serious subjects entertainingly which is perhaps
his greatest gift.

6 TECHNICAL FEATURES

6.1 SOURCES AND ANALOGUES: THE PARDONER

To the present-day reader the way in which the Pardoner takes us into his confidence and reveals his deceptions and greed may be rather puzzling, especially in view of the fact that he later goes on to try to sell his services to his fellow pilgrims. Part of the explanation lies in the fact that Chaucer was using an established convention in having him expose his motives in this way. The closest analogue comes from a long French poem called *Le Roman de la Rose*, which was written in the thirteenth century by Guillaume de Loris and Jean de Meung and translated by Chaucer early in his career. It is a dream poem about love, and takes place in a beautiful garden in which a lover is searching for his lady. He comes across many allegorical figures, including one called Fals-Semblant ('False-Appearance' or 'Hypocrisy'). Fals-Semblant becomes the servant of Love. Fals-Semblant explains that he can be found in many walks of life, secular and religious, not with the poor but with those who are proud and full of crafty tricks, and who eat the best foods and drink good wine. Furthermore he has many different guises. Sometimes he takes on the appearance of a knight or a castle-keeper; at other times he assumes a religious guise and gives easy absolution, without asking too many awkward questions. He goes on (in the Chaucerian translation):

> I wole no lyf but ese and pees,   *want*
> And wynne gold to spende also.
> For whanne the grete bagge is go,   *my purse is empty*
> It cometh right with my japes.
> Make I not wel tumble myn apes?
>   *Don't I make my apes dance well?*

> . . . I wole bothe preche and eke counceilen;
> With hondis wille I not traveilen;
> For of the Pope I have the bulle;
> I ne holde not my wittes dulle.

'What?' asks Love. 'Do you not fear God?'. To which Fals-Semblant replies: 'Certainly not; for you don't often have much success in this world if you fear God'.

Even in the short quoted passage there are verbal parallels with *The Pardoner's Prologue*, and especially with the description in the *General Prologue*, lines 705–6. But it is more important to recognise what Chaucer has apparently done. He seems to have taken a figure who is evil by nature (since the personified abstraction of a sin cannot be good), and who in the *Roman* reveals all because it is the nature of abstractions so to behave (and furthermore he is commanded to do so); he has made Fals-Semblant assume one of his many guises, that of a Pardoner; and he has developed this character partly with regard to how a Pardoner might behave and partly with regard to the hypocrisy and other base qualities of which the source character was an exemplification. It cannot be proved that Chaucer developed the Pardoner in this way, but it seems possible, and at the very least Fals-Semblant must have been in his mind when the characterisation of the Pardoner was beginning to emerge.

6.2 SOURCES AND ANALOGUES: THE TALE

The story of the three *riotoures* is of eastern origin, and the earliest known analogue is one of the *Jatakas*, a third-century Buddhist text. The tale remained popular for many centuries, and one of its most recent appearances is in the form of the story of the king's Ankus in Kipling's *Second Jungle Book* (1895). In the examples which have been located the details sometimes vary but the basic plot remains the same. Several versions survive from around Chaucer's time, mostly in the form of Italian *novelle* (short stories) or in the collections of *exempla* which preachers used as source books for anecdotes with which to enliven their sermons. We do not know from whence Chaucer derived the story, but the version closest to his is in the *Libro di Novelle e di Bel Parlar Gentile*, which was printed in Italy in 1572. The following, however, is from a version more nearly contemporary with *The Pardoner's Tale*, taken from a collection of *exempla* in a manuscript written in Prague in 1406:

A certain hermit was clearing trees to make a vegetable patch, and as he was digging he came by chance upon some treasure. Straightway he cried out in a loud voice, 'Death, death, death!' Just then three friends, who were merchants, happened to pass by, and came to him, saying, 'Where is the death you were shouting about?' So he showed them the treasure, whereupon they immediately drove him off, and he returned to his cell. The merchants, pondering what to do, decided that one of them should go to town for supplies. While that one was away, the others made a plan to kill him on his return as he went down into the hole which had been dug. But he, as he went along, was thinking how he could get rid of the other two. So he got some poison and put it into all the food which he had bought, and on his return said to them, 'Shall we eat first or dig up the treasure?' They said, 'Let's dig up the treasure first', and they got him to go down into the hole. And as he climbed down they killed him. And afterwards they both ate the food and died, so the treasure was left untouched. And when the hermit came there and saw them dead he said, 'Truly, treasure is nothing but danger and death!'

(Translated from the original Latin version printed by W. F. Bryan and G. Dempster, *Sources and Analogues of Chaucer's 'Canterbury Tales'*)

In the analogues the villains either discover the treasure themselves or are directed to it by a character vaguely designated 'a hermit' or 'a philosopher' or 'a wizard' (except in those versions in which the actors are Christ and his disciples). The figure of the old man in *The Pardoner's Tale* seems to have originated somewhere else. Parallels have been noted in an elegy written by the sixth-century Latin Poet Maximian, which contains the sentiments: 'Old age lasts too long . . . I long for death . . . I knock with my staff upon the ground as if asking mother earth to have pity and receive me'. Chaucer's characterisation of the old man may also have been influenced by the widely-popular folktale of the Wandering Jew, who was condemned never to die. Whatever the case, he has skilfully fused these varied themes and ideas to create something fresh and new which far surpasses in literary merit any related work from either before his time or since.

6.3 MEDIEVAL SERMONS

Chaucer would have heard hundreds, and possibly thousands, of sermons in his lifetime, both during his regular attendance at church, which was obligatory for all, and from his experience of occasional preachers such as friars and pardoners, who moved from parish to parish. Friars, and perhaps pardoners too if Chaucer's is anything to go by, were renowned for their lively, anecdotal sermons, and both were frequently in dispute with parish priests, upon whose territory they trespassed and whose roles they usurped. But Chaucer's interest went beyond that of most of his fellow Christians because he was familiar with the complicated theories involved in the art of preaching, and actually wrote several sermons himself – *The Pardoner's Tale* and *The Parson's Tale* are complete sermons and there are sermon-like sections in other poems, such as the discourse on marriage within *The Merchant's Tale*.

The rules of preaching, which were set down in a number of treatises in Chaucer's time, the so-called *Artes Praedicandi* ('Arts of Preaching'), made a distinction between the moral and the technical aspects. The moral rules taught that a preacher is the mouthpiece of the word of God and is not to preach out of aggrandisement or self-satisfaction; in this the Pardoner is clearly at fault. The technical rules taught a complicated rhetoric, the art of effective speaking; and in this the Pardoner excels.

A regular medieval sermon had six distinct sections: the *theme*, or text; the *protheme*, a sort of introduction which was sometimes based on another, related text; the *dilatation*, or exposition of the text; the *exemplum*, or illustration of the theme by reference to incidents or stories; the *peroration*, or application; and the *closing formula*, in the form of a prayer or blessing. The *Pardoner's Prologue* and *Tale*, taken together have three of these ingredients; the text, *Radix malorum est cupiditas*, which is actually referred to as the *theme* (line 333); the *exemplum*, the story of the three *riotoures* through which the moral is conveyed, along with many lesser *exempla*, such as references to Biblical and classical events and authorities (the Pardoner uses the English word *ensaumples* (line 435) to describe these); and the closing formula, with its commendation to the greater pardon of Christ (lines 916–18). Possibly also lines 904–15 might be regarded as a sort of peroration. In addition there are certain characteristic, though not essential, features, such as the *divisio*, the Pardoner's long digression on the tavern sins (483–660). But, despite these affinities, *The Pardoner's Tale* is unlike any real sermon, for it gives too much attention to the main *exemplum* (the story), and too little to the

elaboration of the text itself. The Pardoner's performance is un-
doubtedly shrewd and Chaucer has made him an effective preacher;
but he achieves this rather by *suggesting* a contemporary sermon than
by actually *patterning* the tale upon one.

6.4 RHETORIC

'Rhetoric' in the fourteenth century was the branch of study and
practice which concerned the use of language to persuade through the
employment of an elegant and orderly style. In the preaching
manuals of the time rhetoric features prominently as part of the
codified system of pulpit oratory, the *ars praedicandi*. Chaucer
naturally made use of his considerable skills in rhetoric in all of his
writings, but he is usually skilful enough not to make it obvious. He
makes the Franklin preface his tale with an apology:

> At my bigynnyng first I yow biseche,
> Have me excused of my rude speche.   *unsophisticated*
> I lerned nevere rethorik, certeyn;
> Thyng that I speke, it moot be bare and pleyn. (V. 717–20)

However, *The Franklin's Tale* itself is by no means 'bare and plain' of
rhetorical embellishment. Chaucer's was the art which conceals art,
and it is easy for the present-day reader to get from his work an
impression of simplicity, and even naîvety, which entirely disregards
the skill and craftsmanship which went into constructing his verses. In
fact, Chaucer would not have understood rhetoric as being something
external to be applied to his poetry: to him there would have been
little distinction between 'rhetoric' and 'poetics'.

The Pardoner's Tale, being a sermon, gives particular scope for
rhetorical embellishment, and the 'figures', or 'colours', of rhetoric
are particularly apparent and are emphasised by the Pardoner's
exaggerated style of performance. In describing these here it is
convenient to use some Latin terminology, but we should not be
tyrannised by this, as the terms represent features and effects which
can be described (though less concisely) in other words. The tale
begins by launching straight into the main *exemplum*, the story of the
riotoures. Immediately we notice the figure of *amplificatio* as the
Pardoner takes the word 'folye' (464) and 'amplifies', or expands
upon, it by detailing in the next eighteen lines the particular varieties
of 'folye' in which the band of young revellers are engaged. This leads

to a *sententia*, a generalised statement of traditional wisdom or truth:

luxurie is in wyn and dronkenesse. (484)

This in turn provides a suitable point for a *divisio*, or digression, on the sins of the tavern, which involves *exclamatio* (Lo . . .!), further *exempla* (reference to Lot, Herod, Seneca etc), *apostrophe* (O glotonye . . .!), and *interpretatio*, or saying the same thing in another way (the restatement of *glotony* in lines 498–500 as '*cause first of oure confusion*' and '*original of oure dampnacioun*'). And this leads to another *sententia*:

Corrupt was al this world for glotonye. (504)

Elsewhere the Pardoner uses *hyperbole*, or statement in extreme terms, as when he claims (889–92) that Avicenna never wrote of more certain signs of poisoning than were evident on the bodies of the two villains at the end. Another familiar figure is *onomatopoeia*, making words reflect the sounds of what they describe; an instance is the Pardoner's description of the sound of drunken snoring as being like the words 'Sampsoun, Sampsoun!' (554). Various repetitions also serve to enhance the style, such as the enumeration (*enumeratio*) of the oaths which wicked men swear (651–4), or the repeated *apostrophes* (an example of *anaphora*, that is, beginning successive sentences with the same word), in the lines:

O cursed synne of alle cursednesse!
O traytours homycide, O wikkednesse!
O glotonye, luxurie, and hasardrye! (895–7)

Of course, it is not the case that Chaucer constructed his poem merely by stringing together a series of rhetorical formulae, nor is it a sufficient critical response simply to recognise and describe them. Those who study the poem must be concerned with the effect which is achieved by such things. Most obviously they contribute to the Pardoner's overpowering personal performance. These skills are Chaucer's own, but he had made it appear as if they are those of the Pardoner himself. It is little wonder that the imaginary Pardoner, with such a poet as Chaucer speaking through his mouth, should have had such a devastating power to move and persuade.

6.5 NARRATIVE TECHNIQUE

In contrast to the highly rhetorical digressions, the narrative part of
The Pardoner's Tale is fairly plainly told and the techniques which are
relied upon are those which are characteristic of any good tale of any
age. For instance, the device of contrast is used, most obviously
between the *riotoures* and the old man; direct and indirect speech are
juxtaposed, as in the scene involving the youngest of the villains and
the apothecary; climax is used (the discovery of the gold), along with
anti-climax (the abrupt end to the tale); effective changes of tone
occur (as when the bluster of the *riotoures* turns to furtiveness with
the discovery of the treasure); and suggestive detail is brought in
(such as the 'croked wey' by which the old man directs them to
Death). However, the most impressive narrative feature of *The
Pardoner's Tale* is its pace, which the Pardoner varies with an
unobtrusive sensitivity which is the mark of a master storyteller.

The opening plunges us suddenly into the world of the young
Flemish revellers, whose sins and debauchery are immediately listed in
an awesome catalogue. Exactly who these people are and exactly
what they get up to are no concern of ours; they are there simply to
involve us, to establish for us a foothold in the tale and give the
Pardoner an excuse to launch into his high-sounding digression on the
sins of the tavern. When the story resumes we find ourselves with

Thise riotoures thre of whiche I telle (661)

and off we go again at the same dizzy pace. This unexplained
reference to the three *riotoures*, who have not been mentioned
before, should not puzzle us; sudden leaps such as this are a common
storytelling technique, and the three are introduced so casually that,
even if we do not simply assume that we have already been
introduced, we are happy to accept them as the subjects of the tale
which is now to unfold.

As the story continues we notice that a sense of haste and urgency
is associated with these three men. One of them asks about the
funeral procession outside, speaking curtly to the serving boy, whose
reply is contrastingly measured and polite. A plan is briefly outlined,
and its speedy acceptance taken for granted, while the pledging of
brotherhood is described in a 'perfective' past tense, as if to imply that
it is already over and done:

Togidres han thise thre hir trouthes plight. (702)

The blundering haste of the villains stands in sharp contrast to the calm of the old man whom they now meet. Their terse oaths and threats are entirely unlike the sustained sentences in his long speech. His reluctant explanation of the place where Death can be found is unacknowledged by the *riotoures* as they run pell-mell along the crooked path to the oak tree.

Then a sudden change occurs; with the discovery of the treasure all thoughts of Death evaporate, and the hectic pace moderates, as a sense of cunning wariness creeps in. A pause, and then the ringleader suggests a plan; just as with the earlier plan to swear brotherhood, it is no sooner suggested than accepted, and within three lines the youngest is already on his way to the town to fetch food and drink. The pace slows again, as the ringleader in two long speeches tentatively outlines his treacherous scheme against the one who is away. Meanwhile a wicked plan is even more slowly maturing in the mind of the man on the errand. It is typical of Chaucer (through the Pardoner) to choose this moment (lines 844–8) to slow things down even further by making the theological point that the reason why the devil put this wicked thought into the man's mind was that he found him to be so sinful that he had permission from God to ensnare him (the same point is made at greater length in *The Friar's Tale*, III. 1483–1500). Chaucer's motive for bothering to tell us this may be nothing more than a mischievous desire to delay the outcome. Certainly there is something tantalising in the way he engineers a further delay through the surprisingly detailed description of the young man's conversation with the apothecary and the description of the acquisition and preparation of the bottles. Yet when the end comes it is described swiftly, and the rhetorical figure of *abbrevatio* is used to justify its suddenness:

> What nedeth it to sermone of it moore? (879)

The facts of the deaths are simply stated, and within a few lines the Pardoner is finishing off his performance with a final rhetorical flourish and inviting his audience to come forward and offer to his relics.

6.6 CHARACTERISATION AND NON-CHARACTERISATION

The anonymity and impersonality of the main characters in the tale have already been remarked upon. One commentator has described as 'slightly clumsy and obtrusively impersonal' the way in which

Chaucer refers to the *riotoures* by such terms as 'the first shrewe', 'that oon' and 'that oother'. But whether one agrees or not, it is certainly beyond doubt that Chaucer has gone out of his way to avoid giving them personal identities, and that he has promoted instead aspects of them which are typical. The same is true of the other characters. The old man, to some extent at least, is a representative of old age; his own remarks make this clear, for he uses his own great age to make a general moral point:

> But, sires, to yow it is no curteisye
> To speken to an old man vileynye,
> But he trespasse in word, or elles in dede.
> In Hooly Writ ye may yourself wel rede:
> 'Agayns an oold man, hoor upon his heed,
> Ye sholde arise'; wherfore I yeve yow reed,
> Ne dooth unto an oold man noon harm now,
> Namoore than that ye wolde men did to yow
> In age, if that ye so longe abyde. (739–47)

Similarly, the lesser characters – the serving-boy, the taverner and the apothecary – are included first and foremost to perform their various functions primarily as types, not as individuals. Even Death, who is not a type but a personification, is unexceptional in the way in which he is portrayed, as a 'prive theef' with a spear. However, this general anonymity does not mean that the characters are totally characterless, and certainly not that they are 'flat' and lifeless. The main ways in which this is avoided are by the clever use of dialogue, detail and contrast.

Dialogue accounts for over sixty per cent of the tale proper (that is, from the introduction of 'thise riotoures thre' at line 661). In this part the narrator (whether by this we mean the Pardoner or Chaucer himself) tells the tale almost wholly by means of direct speech and factual narrative. There are only three comments which can be said to express an opinion about the story: one is the reference to their swearing as being like the tearing to pieces of Christ's body (709); the second is the narrator's remark (lines 847–50) that the reason why the devil was able to tempt the poisoner was because he had 'leve' from God to do so; and the third is the judgement at the end (introduced by the words 'I suppose', 889) that Avicenna never wrote of clearer signs of poisoning than were to be seen on the two men who had drunk from the poisoned bottle. Apart from this and from the use of a small number of pejorative terms such as 'the proudeste', 'the worste', 'thise homycides two' and 'the false empoysonere', the men are left to condemn themselves from their own mouths. Their tone ranges from curtness (the command to the serving-boy) to placatory wheedling (the ringleader's persuasion of his fellow to join in the plot against the third), while the matter of their speeches encompasses the swearing of numerous oaths, boasting, gratuitous insult to the old man for no other reason than his great age ('Why lyvestow so longe in so greet age?'), foolish indignation (at the thought that they may be suspected of having stolen the treasure), oath-breaking and conspiracy to murder. All this conveys so strong a sense of depravity that the narrator is able to let the wickedness speak for itself.

Occasional details sometimes assist characterisation. For example, the old man, when confronted by the proudest of the men, 'gan looke in his visage', a small gesture, but one which conveys something of the fearlessness of one who is resigned to and prepared for death. Another example is the information which is slipped in to explain why the poisoner kept a clean bottle of drink for himself:

> For al the nyght he shoop hym for to swynke
> In cariynge of the gold out of that place. (874–5)

There is no real need for this explanation; but it very effectively suggests the greedy anticipation of the man, and by this means adds to the overall dramatic irony (see the following section). The little sketch of the apothecary (whose professional pride is recognisable even in pharmacists of today), the picture of the old man knocking with his staff upon the ground (suggestive both of his desire to return to Mother Earth and, more mundanely, of an ordinary man walking with the aid of a stick), and the way in which the *riotoures* always seem to run, not walk, from place to place – such details as these make up for the general lack of developed characterisation of a more formal and systematic kind.

The use of contrast has something of the same effect, for example between the initial brashness of the *riotoures* and their sly furtiveness once the treasure has been found, or between the master and the serving-boy in the tavern – the one surly and ignorant, the other full of homely wisdom learnt on his mother's knee. But the richest contrasts concern the old man. The critic John Steadman has put these into eight categories: 1. The contrast between youth and age, which is accentuated by the use of terms such as 'us yonge folk' and 'olde cherl'. 2. The contrast between the differing attitudes to death, the one man desiring it, the others seeking to overcome it. 3. The antithetical attitudes to repentance, which develop a theme introduced earlier by the serving-boy, who says of Death:

Beth redy for to meete hym evermoore. (683)

4. The contrast between the wisdom of the old man in his prepared-
ness for death and the foolish ignorance of the *riotoures*, who think
they can overcome Death, and forget him in the enjoyment of the
treasure. 5. The sharply differing attitudes towards the treasure,
which the old man, despite his poverty, has presumably rejected.
6. The contrast between the old man's contempt of the world (a
common medieval theme) and the indulgence of the others in
pleasures which cannot last. 7. The contrast between the old man's
meekness and the ringleader's pride. 8. And finally the old man's
patient acceptance of the misery of man's condition and the others'
quest for Death, whom they are seeking precisely because they do *not*
wish to die.

Clearly these are not characters who exist simply to serve the
unfolding narrative, nor do they have well-developed personalities of
their own; their strength and effectiveness arise rather from the depth
of moral associations and the richness of ironic contrast.

6.7 IRONY

The irony of *The Pardoner's Tale* also needs to be briefly discussed,
although Chaucer's understanding of irony was no different from our
own. Irony then as now involved situations, events and statements
which do not mean what they appear to mean at surface level. The
essence of irony is deception, and those who are its victims often
deserve to be deceived. Irony also depends on point of view, and
since there are potentially many points of view in the case of the
Pardoner and his tale – those of the Pardoner himself, his regular
audience, the pilgrims, the characters in the tale, Chaucer, ourselves
the readers, and perhaps an omniscient moral force beyond us
all – each with a different perception of events, the ingredients are
there for a richly ironic poem, which the *Pardoner's Prologue* and
Tale prove to be.

One level of irony is that which the Pardoner's gullible congregation of 'lewed peple' fails to see. They covet an easy path to heaven
and are therefore susceptible to the Pardoner's tricks. They do not
see that this preacher against drunkenness and the sins of the
ale-house has a personal acquaintance with both; or that in denounc-
ing avarice he grows rich himself; or that he pretends to offer a means
of salvation but in reality does not care if their souls go 'blackber-
rying'; or that his flattery of them covers his deep contempt. His most

successful trick exploits their anxiety not to appear to be secretly unconfessed sinners, and to women he offers an opportunity to make cuckolds of their husbands, while dismissing the husbands' righteous indignation as 'jalousie' (an antifeminist joke common in medieval literature and important in *The Merchant's Tale*). The Pardoner is an evil man and knows how to exploit the evil in others; this is the key to his success. But then, what is 'success'? There are probably not many who would want to be successful in the Pardoner's terms.

The Pardoner's failure to see the limitations of his 'success' is perhaps the overriding irony. He *thinks* he sees things as they are. He describes his motives with a frankness which surprises and shocks. His values are entirely worldly, of course, and in these terms he appears to achieve what he aims for; but even in this respect he is not such a success as he imagines, for Harry Bailly has certainly got the measure of him; he will have nothing to do with the Pardoner or his relics, and puts him in his place, as he rightly deserves. This confrontation with the Host anticipates a much more dreadful meeting when the Pardoner and all men like him who are ruthlessly successful in this world will have to come forward to explain themselves before God. The greatest irony is that the Pardoner and those like him will then be among the damned, while many of those whom they dupe and exploit will be participants in a greater reward than the Pardoner can even contemplate.

The Pardoner's Tale itself is particularly rich in what is known as 'dramatic irony', which occurs when the implications of a speech or event are known to the reader or audience but not to the characters themselves. In the tale the main dramatic irony is that the *riotoures* and the other 'yonge folk' do not see that they are heading for certain damnation. This would be clear to any believing Christian, even without the Pardoner's overt condemnation. But there are more specific examples, one of which is the stupidity of the *riotoures* in failing to understand the nature of Death. Even the humble serving-boy is more informed about this than they are, and, in repeating what his mother taught him, summarises the orthodox doctrine on the subject:

> Me thynketh that it were necessarie
> For to be war of swich an adversarie.
> Beth redy for to meete hym everemoore;
> Thus taughte me my dame; I sey namoore. (681–4)

On the non-literal level this means that people should prepare themselves for death by partaking of the sacraments (especially the sacrament of penance) and by trying to lead decent lives. As if to emphasise the point, the boy's words are taken up by the taverner and rounded off with a further piece of traditional wisdom:

> To been avysed greet wysdom it were,
> Er that he dide a man a dishonour. (690–1)

But the *riotoures* are so stupid that they know none of this, not even, it seems, that in a nearby village Death has carried off every man, woman and child only 'this yeer'. Any audience or reader, and certainly those of Chaucer's time, would be quick to perceive the narrowness of their experience and understanding, and the folly and uselessness of their self-destructive quest. Even their war-cry 'Deeth shal be deed' would have seemed ironically blasphemous to a Chaucerian audience brought up to believe that Christ died on the cross 'that through death He might destroy him that had the power of death, that is, the devil' (St Paul's *Epistle to the Hebrews*, 2:14). In raising this cry, therefore, they call to mind the true victory of Christ over death and the consequent opportunity of eternal life, which they by their behaviour are rejecting.

Another strongly ironic event is their swearing of brotherhood, especially since their resolution to do so is peppered with oaths like 'I make avow to Goddes digne bones' and 'by Goddes dignite'. Obviously their oaths of friendship are no more to be trusted than their other oaths. In view of their murderous plans when they discover the treasure it is ironic that the most specific part of their pledge is

> To lyve and dyen ech of hem for oother. (703)

Moreover, the ringleader, when coaxing his friend to join in the plot against the third, uses terms such as 'my sworen brother', 'oure felawe and 'my deere freend', which ironically remind us of their pact just as they are on the point of breaking it.

The old man's speech, the youngest's anticipated enjoyment of the treasure (revealed to us immediately after the plot upon his own life has been agreed), the murder plans which backfire – all these could be analysed for their ironic content. But to give more examples would be rather like trying to explain a good joke. Every reader brings a different range of experience to bear and is therefore likely to discover ironies that others miss. This is part of the pleasure of reading and rereading *The Pardoner's Tale*.

7 SPECIMEN PASSAGES

7.1 *THE PARDONER'S PROLOGUE*, LINES 329–46

> 'Lordynges,' quod he, 'in chirches whan I preche,
> I peyne me to han an hauteyn speche,   330
> And rynge it out as round as gooth a belle,
> For I kan al by rote that I telle.
> My theme is alwey oon, and evere was –
> *Radix malorum est Cupiditas.*
>   First I pronounce whennes that I come,   335
> And thanne my bulles shewe I, alle and some.
> Oure lige lordes seel on my patente,
> That shewe I first, my body to warente,
> That no man be so boold, ne preest ne clerk,
> Me to destourbe of Cristes hooly werk.   340
> And after that thanne telle I forth my tales;
> Bulles of popes and of cardynales,
> Of patriarkes and bishopes I shewe,
> And in Latyn I speke a wordes fewe,
> To saffron with my predicacioun,   345
> And for to stire hem to devocioun.

Here at the beginning of *The Pardoner's Prologue* he tells us that when he preaches in churches he contrives to adopt 'a lofty, high-sounding manner of speaking', or perhaps simply 'a loud voice' (depending on the meaning of 'hauteyn,' which is not entirely clear). Since he knows it all off by heart he does not have to concern himself with choosing the appropriate words, but rings out his sermon, he says, 'as round as gooth a belle,' that is, 'in tones as rich as those of a bell'. It is difficult to imagine how someone with a high, goat-like voice could achieve this effect, and it may be that he has a false picture of himself, a distortion of vanity.

The Pardoner's Prologue is a self-exposure, and from the start the style is straightforward and revealing, with first personal pronouns (*I, me, my*) very much in evidence. The language is casual and repetitive: 'First I pronounce' . . . 'thanne my bulles shewe I' . . . 'That shewe I first' . . . 'And after that thanne telle I' . . . 'I shewe' . . . 'I speke'. It is almost as if the Pardoner's routine of confidence-trickery is so stereotyped and simple that the most ordinary words will do to describe it.

One *theme* (i.e. sermon text) suffices for all occasions – St Paul's famous maxim *Radix malorum est Cupiditas*, 'Desire for money is the root of evil'; later the Pardoner explains why this is specially appropriate, for *Cupiditas* is his own favourite vice. This sonorous-sounding text is intended to impress, as are the credentials he shows at the start of his act – bulls issued by 'popes, cardinals, patriarchs and bishops' (he has the lot), and the letter patent bearing what he claims to be the bishop's seal (all of which, being in Latin, would have been totally incomprehensible to the ordinary people, who probably would not have been able even to read English). His over-insistence on all this makes us suspect fraud, but the ignorant multitude was not so suspicious, and by the time he had thrown in a few more impressive-sounding Latin phrases they were no doubt totally captivated.

Despite the fundamentally simple style, room is found for a few embellishments, such as the simile 'as round as gooth a belle' and the metaphorical phrase 'to saffron with my predicacioun,' 'with which to add spice to my sermon', which utilises the imagery of *haute cuisine*, something the Pardoner later denounces. There is a sprinkling of technical terms ('bulles, patente, warente'), as well as tags ('alle and some', 'ne preest ne clerk'), which are useful both as line-fillers and as a means of creating the impression of ordinary speech. Finally, it is worth pointing out how beautifully the text *Radix malorum est Cupiditas* fits Chaucer's pentameter line.

7.2 *THE PARDONER'S TALE*, LINES 549–88

> A lecherous thing is wyn, and dronkenesse
> Is ful of stryvyng and of wrecchednesse.   550
> O dronke man, disfigured is thy face,
> Sour is thy breeth, foul artow to embrace,
> And thurgh thy dronke nose semeth the soun

As though thou seydest ay 'Sampsoun, Sampsoun!'
And yet, God woot, Sampsoun drank nevere no wyn.   555
Thou fallest as it were a styked swyn;
Thy tonge is lost, and al thyn honeste cure;
For dronkenesse is verray sepulture
Of mannes wit and his discrecioun.
In whom that drynke hath dominacioun   560
He kan no conseil kepe, it is no drede.
Now kepe yow fro the white and fro the rede,
And namely fro the white wyn of Lepe,
That is to selle in Fysshstrete or in Chepe.
This wyn of Spaigne crepeth subtilly   565
In othere wynes, growynge faste by,
Of which ther ryseth swich fumositee
That whan a man hath dronken draughtes thre,
And weneth that he be at hoom in Chepe,
He is in Spaigne, right at the toune of Lepe –
Nat at the Rochele, ne at Burdeux toun;   571
And thanne wol he seye 'Sampsoun, Sampsoun!'
   But herkneth, lordynges, o word, I yow preye,
That alle the sovereyn actes, dar I seye,
Of victories in the Olde Testament,   575
Thurgh verray God, that is omnipotent,
Were doon in abstinence and in preyere.
Looketh the Bible, and ther ye may it leere.
   Looke, Attila, the grete conquerour,   579
Deyde in his sleep, with shame and dishonour,
Bledynge ay at his nose in dronkenesse.
A capitayn sholde lyve in sobrenesse.
And over al this, avyseth yow right wel
What was comaunded unto Lamuel –
Nat Samuel, but Lamuel, seye I;   585
Redeth the Bible, and fynde it expresly
Of wyn-yevyng to hem that han justise.
Namoore of this, for it may wel suffise.

This attack on drunkenness is part of the Pardoner's digression on
the tavern sins, which he embarks upon as soon as he has set the
scene for his tale but before he turns his attention specifically to the
three *riotoures*. It is eloquent and forceful oratory, and achieves its
effect largely by the use of well-known figures of rhetoric. The
pattern is typical: It begins with a *sententia*, a short, pithy statement

expressing a general truth; in this case it has Biblical authority, for it is borrowed from the Book of Proverbs (20:1):

> A lecherous thyng is wyn, and dronkenesse
> Is ful of stryvyng and of wrecchednesse.

Utilising the figure of direct address called *apostrophe* '(O dronke man), the Pardoner then supports this general point by introducing more detailed evidence, including a catalogue (*enumeratio*) of the unpleasant side-effects of drinking (disfigured face, stinking breath, foulness in embrace etc), which in turn makes use of the device of *onomatopoeia* ('Sampsoun, Sampsoun!' to suggest the sound of deep snoring). And shortly we are brought to another *sententia*:

> For dronkenesse is verray sepulture
> Of mannes wit and his discrecioun,

which is another proverb (though this time not Biblical), effectively summing up the argument and enabling the Pardoner to proceed, with a slight change of direction, to his specific warning against red and white wine. This ends with the reiteration of the *onomatopoeic* 'Sampsoun, Sampsoun!', which leads neatly back to the general line of argument. Then follows a series of *exempla* – the soberly obtained victories of the Old Testmant, the shameful death of Attila, God's prohibition to Lemuel – by which time the Pardoner senses that his point has been made, and finishes with a rather summary *abbrevatio*:

> Namoore of this, for it may wel suffise.

The Pardoner's *exempla* here are quite different from the main *exemplum* of the three *riotoures*; these are passing allusions to people and events so well known as to require the minimum of elaboration (in the Pardoner's opinion, at least). Everyone knows, he implies, that all the famous victories of the Old Testament were achieved in a spirit of sobriety and prayer; everyone knows that Attila, the cruel King of the Huns, died a shameful death by choking of a bleeding nose as he lay in a drunken stupor on his wedding night; and everyone knows that Lemuel was taught that kings and princes should not drink wine lest they lose their wits and pervert the law. All the same, his sweeping admonitions 'looketh the Bible' and 'redeth the Bible' (which are not characteristic of real sermons, which always at that time gave copious and exact Biblical references) imply a deficiency of real knowledge, which is so often a mark of those whose little wisdom is learned parrot-fashion.

Underlying the Pardoner's oratory is a strain of ridiculous posturing. His insistence on the distinction between *Lamuel* and *Samuel*, for instance, is absurdly pedantic. His exaggerated and perhaps pompous style is undermined by ordinary-sounding tags like 'God woot', 'it is no drede' and 'dar I seye'. A sense of bathos (demeaning inappropriateness) arises from the contrast between style and content – after all, are bad breath and snoring *really* fit subjects for a style so overwrought as this? And does the complicated, and probably topical, in-joke about the illicit mixing of cheap Spanish wines with the more expensive French varieties (amusing as it is) really belong here? Or has Chaucer introduced it mischievously to imply that the hypocrite Pardoner has a greater knowledge of Fish Street and Cheapside hostelries than is appropriate to one of his profession and of his professed moral standards? Certainly the true character of the Pardoner can be discerned beneath the veneer of moral respectability if only we look closely enough.

7.3 *THE PARDONER'S TALE*, LINES 750–72

'Nay, olde cherl, by God, thou shalt nat so,'
Seyde this oother hasardour anon;
'Thou partest nat so lightly, by Seint John!
Thou spak right now of thilke traytour Deeth,
That in this contree alle oure freendes sleeth.
Have heer my trouthe, as thou art his espye,
Telle where he is, or thou shalt it abye,
By God, and by the hooly sacrement!
For soothly thou art oon of his assent
To sleen us yonge folk, thou false theef!'
'Now, sires,' quod he, 'if that yow be so leef
To fynde Deeth, turne up this croked wey,
For in that grove I lafte hym, by my fey,
Under a tree, and there he wole abyde;
Noght for youre boost he wole him no thyng
    hyde.
Se ye that ook? Right there ye shal hym
    fynde.
God save yow, that boghte agayn mankynde,
And yow amende! Thus seyde this olde man;
And ever rich of thise riotoures ran

Til he cam to that tree, and ther they founde
Of floryns fyne of gold ycoyned rounde
Wel ny an eighte busshels, as hem thoughte.
No lenger thanne after Deeth they soughte.

The passage illustrates Chaucer's technique of storytelling by dialogue. It also shows very clearly how the device of contrast is used in the tale, in this case between one of the *riotoures* (the one who has been referred to as 'the proudeste' and the 'oold man and a povre' whom they meet on their quest to find Death.

The younger man is described as 'this oother hasardour'; the Chaucerian idiom means 'this other man, the gambler'. The word 'hasardour' here seems virtually synonymous with *riotoure*, except that it is more specific; it links up with the general condemnation of 'hasardrye' in the Pardoner's digression, and it fits in with the ringleader's later plan to 'pleye at dees right at oure owene wille'. The man's speech is full of oaths ('by God', 'by Seint John', 'by the hooly sacrement'), which hark back to another part of the Pardoner's condemnatory digression. Other characteristics of low speech indicative of his depraved character are terms of abuse ('olde cherl', 'thou false theef'), asseveration ('have heer my trouthe'), emphatic contradictions ('thou shalt nat so', 'thou partest nat so lightly'), threats ('thou shalt it abye'), and disparagement ('thilke traytour Deeth'). The only relief from this is the reference to the 'freendes' whom Death has taken, by which the man seeks to imply that their drunken chase after Death is for the public good. The overall tone of the speech, then, is coarse and intimidating.

In contrast, the old man replies politely, calling them 'sires' and using the impersonal construction 'if that yow be so leef'. There is a sense of reluctance in the directions he gives, and we assume that in his wisdom he knows the inevitable fatal outcome of their quest. His speech contains some uncanny details ('this croked wey', 'that ook'), which hint at a significance not easy to define. Could the 'croked wey' symbolise the wrongness of the course they are following? And, if the treasure is in so specific a spot, who put it there, and why? The old man's speech, like that of the other man, also contains emphatic phrases and asseverations ('by my fey', 'no thyng'), and he makes assertions as strongly as the other ('he wole abyde', 'he wole him no thyng hyde'); but these are couched in moderate terms, and his parting invocation of God (in contrast to the other's) is in the form of a blessing.

There is dramatic irony in this parting blessing, for the reference to 'God . . . that boghte, agayn mankynde' reminds us of Christ's death on the cross, by means of which (according to basic Christian doctrine) a course of salvation was made available to all those who repent. The parting prayer that God may 'amende' them is therefore doubly ironic, since when death comes all opportunity for 'amendment' will be past. But the men cast this advice aside and 'run' to the oak tree. Their discovery there of the gold marks a turning point, as, breathless from the running, they are stopped in their tracks by the sight of all that beautiful treasure. The florins are in mint condition ('fyne'), and every aspect of them seems to be savoured by the men – even their roundness. We are not told that there were 'an eighte busshels' of them (an enormous quantity, for a bushel is a capacity measure of eight gallons, more appropriate to wheat or fruit than to golden coins), but that this is what 'it seemed to them' ('hem thoughte'); in this way we are taken into their minds, from which all thoughts of their quest have ironically vanished.

8 CRITICAL RECEPTION

A convenient anthology of Chaucer criticism over nearly six hundred years is J. A. Burrow's *Geoffrey Chaucer* (Penguin Critical Anthologies, 1969). A useful summary is the chapter entitled 'Images of Chaucer 1386–1900' in *Chaucer and the Chaucerians*, edited by D. S. Brewer (Nelson, 1966). The reader is referred to these for information on the changing attitudes to Chaucer over the years. This section will concentrate specifically on the Pardoner.

We do not hear much of the Pardoner in the writings of the fifteenth and sixteenth centuries, though Roger Ascham, sometime tutor to Princess Elizabeth, later Elizabeth I, refers to *The Pardoner's Tale* in his *Toxophilus* (1544). Dealing with gambling, he writes that its

> horriblenes is so large that it passed the eloquence of our Englische Homer [i.e. Chaucer] to compass it: yet because I euer thought hys sayinges to have as much authoritye as eyther Sophocles or Euripedes in Greke, therefore gladly do I remember these verses of hys,

and he goes on to quote lines 591–4 of the *Pardoner's Tale*, inserting a moral disquisition on the points raised in each line.

A more telling sign of interest in *The Pardoner's Prologue* and *Tale* is the imitations they inspired in these early years. One of the best known is by the Tudor dramatist John Heywood (c. 1497–c. 1580), whose *Merry Play between the Pardoner and the Friar, the Curate and Neighbour Pratt* was printed in 1533; for the Pardoner's opening speech Heywood blatantly plagiarises Chaucer's *Pardoner's Prologue*:

Our liege Lord seal here on my patent
I bear with me my body to warrant;
That no man be so bold, be he priest or clerk,
Me to disturb of Christ's holy wark . . .

And so he embarks upon the routine familiar to us from Chaucer, which is then extended with newly invented preposterous relics, such as the big toe of the Holy Trinity, the jawbone of All-Hallows, and the brain-pan of St Michael. Shortly afterwards a Friar begins a rival sermon, and the two eventually fall to blows.

The Scottish playwright Sir David Lindsay (1490–1555) probably used much the same source of inspiration for the interlude of the Pardoner which he introduced into his *Satyre of the Thrie Estaits*, which was acted at court in 1540. In this case a Pardoner sets out his pardons and a motley selection of false relics, including the right jawbone of Finn mac Coul, a legendary Gaelic hero 'with teith and al togidder', the horn of old Colin's cow, and the long rope which was used to hang the notorious criminal Johnnie Armstrong. But this is a post-Reformation Pardoner, and times are hard for him, because, as he says, the abuses perpetrated by members of his profession are now common knowledge:

Bot now, alace, our griet abusioun
Is cleirly knawin, til our confusioun;   *to*
That we may sair repent.   *sorely*
Of all credence now I am quyte,   *empty*
For ilk man halds me at dispyte.   *every*

After the sixteenth century the Pardoner is not singled out for particular mention of note until the nineteenth. A well-known comment of this time is by the poet and artist William Blake, who admired Chaucer and painted portraits of the Canterbury pilgrims. In *A Descriptive Catalogue of Pictures, Poetical and Historical Inventions*, published in 1809, Blake writes:

But I have omitted to speak of a very prominent character, the Pardoner, the Age's Knave, who always commands and domineers over the high and low vulgar. This man is sent in every age for a rod and scourge, and for a blight, for a trial of men, to divide the classes of men . . .

A sign of the continuing interest in the Pardoner in the first half of the nineteenth century is the translation of the tale made by the

Victorian poet Leigh Hunt, which appeared in 1845 under the title *Death and the Ruffians*. It begins

> In Flanders once there liv'd a company
> Of foolish youth, a lawless set of three,
> That, haunting every place of foul repute,
> And giddy with the din of harp and lute,
> Went dancing, and sat dicing, day and night,
> And eat and drank beyond their nature's might
> And thus upon the devil's own altar laid
> The bodies and the souls that God had made.

In translating Chaucer, Hunt is following the example of another famous poet of the previous century, John Dryden (though *The Pardoner's Tale* was not amongst those at which Dryden tried his hand). In this case the translation serves only to emphasise the robust brilliance of the original.

By the end of the century more attention was being given to the individual works of Chaucer, and *The Pardoner's Tale* was one of those which commanded attention. It was at this time that the pervasive strain of criticism began to develop which responds to the opportunity to probe the psychology of the Pardoner. In his essay 'Chaucer's Pardoner' (1893) the American scholar G. L. Kittredge expressed the belief that he could detect in the Pardoner's commendation of his audience to the greater pardon of Christ ('For that is best; I wol yow nat deceyve'), a glimmer of his 'better nature, which he had himself thought dead long ago'. W. C. Curry in *Chaucer and the Medieval Sciences* (1926) extended this rationalisation of the Pardoner's character by referring to the medieval pysiognomy books, and came to the conclusion that by this means he could identify him as a congenital eunuch 'provided by nature with a warped mind and soul'; this he described as 'the Pardoner's secret', almost as if he were a real person. Both these lines of thought have been influential and have been expanded upon in subsequent criticism, though the dangers of taking this too far are now recognised.

Psychological analysis has also featured in attempts to explain the Pardoner's damaging self-exposure and his strange and unsuccessful attempt to get the pilgrims to offer to his relics. Derek Pearsall in *The Canterbury Tales* (1985) amusingly summarises some of the explanations which have been suggested:

> He is on holiday and does not expect to meet these people in the future course of business; he is dazzled by the chance to show off in

such comparatively distinguished company; he is drunk and does not know what he is doing; he is offended by the unwillingness of the *gentils* to allow him to tell a tale of *myrthe* and therefore deliberately gives them an exaggerated version of the diabolical degenerate of their imaginings so that they will realise their mistake and see him as a good-natured rogue by contrast . . . he is joking wildly because he is ashamed of having given way to a momentary spasm of sincerity; he is in earnest; he is momentarily in earnest, having been carried away by his own tale; he sees the pilgrims carried away by his tale and seizes the chance to make the most spectacular and unlooked-for *coup*.

Pearsall goes on:

Some of these explanations are of course naïve by any standards, and look for a literalness in the rendering of dramatic situation which would be inappropriate in most literary contexts, and which is specially inappropriate in the context of a 'performance' like the Pardoner's . . . At the same time, the impact the Pardoner makes as a character, and as an individual, must be acknowledged. Convention has its place, and psychologically realistic interpretation its excesses, but a special quality of power, of evil, of death, is too strong in the Pardoner, and too universally apprehended, to allow him to be easily fitted into a set medieval literary convention.

The following are some other worthwhile comments on the Pardoner and his *Tale*:

The Three Rioters, seeking Death in order to slay him, find him without knowing that it is he, and are themselves slain by their own motive principle, cupidity. The personal situation of the Pardoner himself is equally ironical. It has often been said he is a lost soul, but he is more; he is a lost soul peddling a fake salvation for other souls, as if all salvation were a fake. Like Iago he knows all the right things to say, and says them for his private ends. The irony is that they are true while he supposes them a mockery.

(Nevil Coghill, *The Poet Chaucer*)

The huge power of the impression of that old man seems to proceed from the sense that he is more – or at least other – than a personal old man; that he possesses a non-human as well as a human force; that he seems 'to recede from us into some more powerful life'. Though it is not said who he is, he has the original force of the allegorical Age (Elde). As Age he is connected with Death, comes as a warning of Death, knows about Death and where he is to be found . . . The old man therefore knows more, is more powerful for all his apparent meekness and frailty than the proudest of the rioters who foolishly addresses him as inferior and who may be supposed to shrink from the suggested exchange of his youth for the old man's age.

(John Speirs, *Chaucer the Maker*)

The high-flown rhetoric of the sermon, in the context of the self-revelation of the monologue, produces a mock-effect which satirises the canned fireworks of the professional preachers. Chaucer underlines this effect by making the rhetorical outbursts glaringly ornamental, so that our attention is transferred from the meaning of the speech to the manipulations of the speaker.

(Charles Muscatine in *Chaucer and the Chaucerians*,
edited by D. S. Brewer)

No work of Chaucer's could more easily have become a document of decadence than his *Pardoner's Tale*. It contains the depth of cynicism, the dwelling of fleshly corruption, the vulgarised allegory, the crudity, and the tastelessness of the late Gothic style. Yet none of these traits is finally gratuitous or uncontrolled. Each is held in perspective: circumscribed by the larger scheme of the *Tales*, subsumed in the characterisation of the Pardoner, bounded by the amicable ending, redeemed by the admission

> And Jhesu Christ, that is our soules leche,
> So graunte yow his pardoun to receyve,
> For that is best.

The tale, while it explores the outermost limits of the medieval moral order, still proclaims the integrity of that order.

(Charles Muscatine, *Chaucer and the French Tradition*)

REVISION QUESTIONS

1. Is the portrait of the Pardoner in the *General Prologue* consistent with the details of him which emerge from his *Prologue* and *Tale*?

2. 'He was in chirche a noble ecclesiaste' (*General Prologue*, line 708). How can Chaucer say such a thing of a man as depraved as the Pardoner?

3. 'The Pardoner is not portrayed realistically or given any psychological depth.' Discuss.

4. Examine the view that the Pardoner is a more extreme example of depravity than any which he describes in his tale.

5.   But though myself be gilty in that synne,
         Yet kan I maken oother folk to twynne
         From avarice, and soore to repente.

   Do these lines, or anything else in *the Pardoner's Prologue* and *Tale*, suggest that there is a substratum of sincerity in the Pardoner's performance?

6. Describe the Pardoner's technique for making money.

7. Describe the nature and effectiveness of the Pardoner's rhetoric.

8. How effective is *The Pardoner's Tale* as a sermon?

9. What use is made of irony in *The Pardoner's Tale*?

10. Describe and illustrate some of the narrative qualities in the story of the three *riotoures* in *The Pardoner's Tale*.

11. What is the meaning and function of the old man in *The Pardoner's Tale*?

12. Consider some of the possible explanations of the Pardoner's offer to the pilgrims at the end of his tale. Which of these do you find the most convincing?

13. '*The Pardoner's Prologue* and *The Pardoner's Tale* form an inseparable unit; without the one the value and impact of the other would be immeasurably decreased.' Discuss.

14. '*The Pardoner's Prologue* and *The Pardoner's Tale* demonstrate Chaucer's ability to treat serious subjects entertainingly.' Discuss.

FURTHER READING

Editions

Cawley, A. C., *Geoffrey Chaucer: Canterbury Tales*, 2nd edn (Dent, Everyman's Library, 1975)

Coghill, Nevill, and Christopher Tolkien, *Chaucer: The Pardoner's Tale* (Harrap, 1958)

Havely, N. R., *The Friar's, Summoner's and Pardoner's Tales from the Canterbury Tales* (University of London Press, 1975)

Robinson, F. N., *The Works of Geoffrey Chaucer*, 2nd edn (Oxford University Press, 1957)

Spearing, A. C., *The Pardoner's Prologue and Tale* (Cambridge University Press, 1965)

Robinson's is still the standard edition but is beginning to show its age; a third edition is in preparation. Cawley's has a marginal glossary, which makes it a good choice for anyone coming to read *The Canterbury Tales* in the original for the first time. The best edition specifically of *The Pardoner's Prologue and Tale* is that of Coghill and Tolkien, though all have much to commend them, including excellent notes and commentary.

Translations

Coghill, Nevill, *Chaucer: The Canterbury Tales*, 3rd edn (Penguin, 1960)

Wright, David, *Chaucer: The Canterbury Tales: A Modern Prose Rendering* (Panther, 1965)

Coghill's translation, which is in verse, is the more widely known and used.

Background

Brewer, Derek, *Chaucer and his World* (Eyre Methuen, 1978)

Brewer, Derek, *English Gothic Literature* (Macmillan, 1983)

Hussey, Maurice, *Chaucer's World: A Pictorial Companion* (Cambridge University Press, 1967)

Handbooks and Introductions to Chaucer

Brewer, Derek, *Chaucer in his Time* (Nelson, 1963)

Brewer, Derek, *Chaucer*, 3rd edn (Longman, 1973)

Burnley, David, *A Guide to Chaucer's Language* (Macmillan, 1983)

Hussey, Maurice, A. C. Spearing and James Winny, *An Introducion to Chaucer* (Cambridge University Press, 1965)

Rowland, Beryl (ed), *Companion to Chaucer Studies* (Oxford University Press, 1968)

Ford, Boris (ed), *The New Pelican Guide to English Literature, vol 1, Medieval Literature: Part 1: Chaucer and the Alliterative Tradition; Part 2: The European Inheritance* (Penguin 1982/3)

Criticism

Coghill, Nevill, *The Poet Chaucer*, 2nd edn (Oxford University Press, 1967)

Elliott, Ralph W. V., *The Nun's Priest's Tale and the Pardoner's Tale* (Blackwell, 1965)

Faulkner, D. R. (ed), *The Pardoner's Tale: A Collection of Critical Essays* (Prentice-Hall, 1973)

Mann, Jill, *Chaucer and Medieval Estates Satire* (Cambridge University Press, 1973)

Pearsall, Derek, *The Canterbury Tales* (George Allen and Unwin, 1985)

Schoeck, Richard J., and Jerome Taylor (eds), *Chaucer Criticism, vol. 1: The Canterbury Tales* (University of Notre Dame Press, 1960)

Speirs, John, *Chaucer the Maker,* 2nd edn (Faber, 1960)

Wagenknecht, Edward (ed), *Chaucer: Modern Essays in Criticism* (Oxford University Press, 1959)

Mann's book deals specifically with the *General Prologue*. Schoeck and Taylor's and Wagenknecht's are anthologies, both of which contain an essay by G. G. Sedgewick which surveys scholarship on the *Pardoner's Prologue* and *Tale* between the years 1880 and 1940, when views which are current today were beginning to evolve; Pearsall's section on the Pardoner extends the survey more or less to the present day.

Records and tapes

Chaucer: Prologue to the Canterbury Tales, read by Nevill Coghill, Norman Davis and John Burrow. Argo RG 401. (LP)

Geoffrey Chaucer, read by Nevill Coghill and Norman Davis. BOW.
  (LP includes *The Pardoner's Tale*)
*Two Canterbury Tales in Middle English: The Pardoner's Prologue
  and Tale, and The Nun's Priest's Tale*, read by Robert Ross.
  Caedmon TC 1008 (LP); CDL 51008 (cassette)
The Pardoner's Prologue and Tale, read by Richard Bebb and others.
  Issued as a double cassette pack with the reading of the *General
  Prologue* (Argo RG 401, above). Argo SAY 24.
Chaucer: *The Nun's Priest's Tale* and *The Pardoner's Tale* [discussed
  by] Derek Brewer and A. C. Spearing. Audio Learning ELA 019
  (cassette).

Mastering English Literature

Richard Gill

Mastering English Literature will help readers both to enjoy English Literature and to be successful in 'O' levels, 'A' levels and other public exams. It is an introduction to the study of poetry, novels and drama which helps the reader in four ways - by providing ways of approaching literature, by giving examples and practice exercises, by offering hints on how to write about literature, and by the author's own evident enthusiasm for the subject. With extracts from more than 200 texts, this is an enjoyable account of how to get the maximum satisfaction out of reading, whether it be for formal examinations or simply for pleasure.

Work Out English Literature ('A' level)

S.H. Burton

This book familiarises 'A' level English Literature candidates with every kind of test which they are likely to encounter. Suggested answers are worked out step by step and accompanied by full author's commentary. The book helps students to clarify their aims and establish techniques and standards so that they can make appropriate responses to similar questions when the examination pressures are on. It opens up fresh ways of looking at the full range of set texts, authors and critical judgements and motivates students to know more of these matters.